D0108646

religious ferment in asia

Central Bible College Library
Springfield, Missouri

Studies on Asia, Second Series (Volume II–1969)
Grant K. Goodman, General Editor

Religious Ferment in Asia

55136

Edited by Robert J. Miller

Central Bible College Library
Springfield, Missouri

THE UNIVERSITY PRESS OF KANSAS/LAWRENCE/MANHATTAN/WICHITA

© Copyright 1974 by the University Press of Kansas
Printed in the United States of America
Designed by Fritz Reiber

Library of Congress Cataloging in Publication Data

Miller, Robert James 1923–   comp.
Religious ferment in Asia.

(Studies on Asia, 2d ser., v. 2)
"Most of the papers . . . were originally presented at the Midwestern Conference on Asian Studies (1969)."
1. Asia—Religion—Addresses, essays, lectures.
I. Midwest Conference on Asian Affairs, 18th, Oklahoma State University, Stillwater, 1969.
II. Title. II. Series.
DS2.S8 2dser., vol. 2 [BL1035]   915'.008s
ISBN 0-7006-0111-2   [200'.95]   73-11401

EDITOR'S FOREWORD

> For many years investigators attempted to create *elegant* theories, descriptions, and systems definitions. . . . The aim was to obtain a neat, apt, fastidious selection. . . . The concept of elegance conflicts with the facts of life in many systems, which can be inherently messy. To eliminate such "messiness" in the name of simplicity destroys one of the essential characteristics of the system to be defined.[1]

The system under consideration here is religion, notoriously a difficult subject for analysis and one whose essential characteristics are still debated. At times our authors attempt to explain processes that may have their beginnings in the minds of individuals, that unfold in the interplay of movements and ideas, or that result in conflict between segments of some system. At such times the inherent complexity—messiness—of the system or systems under discussion becomes evident.

In this volume we seek to illustrate essential characteristics of a system or systems in ferment, in the broad area of Asia. There is no overriding theoretical or disciplinary framework imposed to simplify the complexity that results. Religion shades into politics; secular actions share boundaries with religious actions in apparent or momentary identity; individuals and groups manipulate, codify, and exemplify symbols drawn from

1. Van Court Hare, *Systems Analysis: A Diagnostic Approach*, Harbrace Series in Business & Economics (New York, 1967), pp. 155–56.

the popular, visceral "religious" beliefs of their time. Always the focus is on religion, however; our contributors avoid the temptation to venture off into general discussions of social, political, or economic change per se.

Surprisingly, considering that most of the papers in this volume were originally presented at the Midwestern Conference on Asian Studies (1969), certain emphases appear at the very beginning that suggest an underlying unity of approaches among the authors. Themes set forth in the Introduction are elaborated in part or whole by other authors. The politicalization of religious values and organizations is one such theme; another lies in the disparate reactions of urbanizing and of rural populations toward attempts to modify the traditional patterns of life, or in their views of what really constitutes tradition. An associated theme is the simplification of traditional religious doctrine, a process accelerated by the use of contemporary technology and media. Some themes, subsidiary in the Introduction, are more fully developed in subsequent papers. Two such themes are, in fact, the subjects of whole essays: the selective use of tradition by renewing or revitalizing movements; and the process by which religious imperatives become viewed and used as secular ethics, understood as nothing more than the facts of life.

The prevalence of these various themes throughout a set of conference papers is certainly not the result of "neat, apt, fastidious selection." It suggests either extraordinary prescience on the part of the participants, or perhaps an underlying grasp of the "essential characteristics of the system" under observation. The organization of the papers emerges naturally, even though it is produced deliberately. From individuals acting as distillers of fermented ideas, we move to the products of fermentation—distillations—as seen in movements, organizations, and part-societies, some becoming in turn distillers of ferment, producing new ferment. At the end of each section we present a paper posing a general theoretical approach to some of the problems raised in the section. In each section we explore examples of agitated, obvious ferment, and of quiet, slow, sometimes non-visible ferment. As our Introduction so aptly puts it, we must include *both* within our system as we seek to define it, for unless we are able to see the ferment sometimes hidden in apparent stability, "we will all too often see religious ferment where there is only momentary agitation without ultimate significance; and we will run the risk of failing to discern the significant ferment that frequently, in a quiet fashion, renews the traditional while incorporating the new and modern into itself."

Robert J. Miller
New Delhi
August 1971

CONTENTS

1

Introduction

Religious Ferment in Asia

Philip H. Ashby
Princeton University

For even the casual observer of the world today there are certain obvious generalizations that can be made about our subject—Religious Ferment in Asia. For a group of scholars—people who are anything but casual about the matter—there is an awareness of the danger of generalizations, a well-founded skepticism of them, and yet, I would think, an appreciation of the part that well-informed generalizations can play in the scholarly endeavor to comprehend a vast and complex subject. Formulations of the generalizations and the attempt to justify them by concrete examples, criticism of them and citation of exceptions, or, more devastatingly, reference to strongly contradictory facts or trends and therefore a resulting direct attack upon the broad statements that we are all prone to make—all of these taken together are integral parts of the attempt to gain a disciplined understanding.

Even in the matter of the words "Religious Ferment," the theme of this collection, we should devote attention to just what we mean to convey by these words. When we speak of "the religious" in reference to Asia, do we mean what is now so often referred to as the amalgam of the great and little traditions of a particular cultural-social area of Asia? By the word "religious" are we focusing attention upon the seminal themes inherent to the philosophical-theological *Weltanschauung* together with the folk cult as the two mingle in a relationship that often appears ambiguous and even contradictory to the essential nature of each? And what about the norms of the social structure, the idealized ways of behavior, and the custom moralities: Are

---

Diacritical marks have not been used consistently by the several contributors; and they have not been used in some Sanskrit words because the printer did not have them.

these included in our term in a deliberate meaningful manner; are they merely assumed to be included without specific attention being paid to them; or, perhaps, are they excluded because our particular theoretical definition of the religious and our resulting methodology consider them at most to be peripheral to our concern?

There would appear to be little problem with the word "ferment" and what we mean by it. Certainly the cultures and the societies of the nation states of Asia are in ferment along with most if not all of the rest of the world, and perhaps more so. That is to say the obvious: namely, that they are agitated by the conditions of their surroundings and are excited by the events of this time in their history.

However, when we put the two words together, when we qualify "ferment" by the adjective "religious," a new and not so demonstrable generalization is suggested. Are the traditional religions associated with the cultures and societies of Asia agitated? Are they excited? If so, to what degree and why; if not, how are they accurately described? And, in either case—in ferment or not—what is their present role or roles in the ferment that we probably agree surrounds them today? Are they conservative forces fighting a losing battle in defense of the traditional values of the particular area; are they enlightened and adaptive preservers of past riches, seeking to incorporate that wealth into newly emerging modes and structures; or are they merely passive observers of the ferment that surrounds them?

Quite by accident, recently I read or reread in just the space of a few hours one morning the following assessments of three leading Asian religions. In his autobiography, Bertrand Russell reprinted an article that he wrote during his tour of China in 1920, in which he said: "Chinese religion is curiously cheerful. When one arrives at a temple, they give one a cigarette and a cup of delicately fragrant tea. . . . Buddhism, which one thinks of as ascetic, is here quite gay. The saints have fat stomachs, and are depicted as people who thoroughly enjoy life. No one seems to believe the religion, not even the priests."[1] I am certain that there are many Asian scholars who, while not being able to get into China, have had similar experiences in Japan in recent years and would have been tempted to write about Buddhism in Japan as Russell did about it in China, if they had not plumbed deeper into the religious situation of Japan.

Or, coming closer to the present, in 1961, while in prison

under sentence of death, Mohammad Fadhel Jamali, former foreign minister and prime minister of Iraq, wrote a series of letters to his son concerning Islamic faith and practice. To quote just a brief passage: "The Islamic society, then, is retarded in understanding the Islamic creed, in performing Islamic duties, in following Islamic legislation, and in practising sublime Islamic morality. The reason for this goes back to defects in general and public education, defects in the home, the school, the men of religion, the leaders and guides—all are responsible for the true Islamic education of Moslems, but they have mostly failed in their duties."[2] Here also, I am sure, there are many of us who on the basis of first-hand experience and serious study would give a similar estimate of the Muslim situation.

Or, even more recently, speaking about India and Hinduism, the eminent Hindu scholar R. N. Dandekar said: "Today, India, like the rest of the world, is witnessing a major conflict of values. In India, as elsewhere, there is a distinct shift of interest. . . . In the matter of religion, the Hindus have now generally become listless. They are merely drifting. . . . The first and foremost requisite in this connection is to banish the prevailing atmosphere of frustration and cynicism."[3] Again, as is the case in Buddhist and Muslim areas of Asia, all who know Hinduism well are aware of the listless and drifting aspects of contemporary Hinduism to which Dandekar refers.

But of course we cannot simply stop at this point. We cannot trust the easily made generalization of a foreign lay observer made decades ago about Buddhism in China. And despite our respect for their first-hand insights, we cannot and must not isolate the negative remarks of leading adherents of the major religions of the Asian world and thereby ignore the main thrust of their statements of faith in the enduring values of their traditional religions. The situation is changing too rapidly for us to depend upon anything but the latest information, and strongly negative or positive judgments must be weighed carefully in light of the many exceptions that may very well prove to be the rule rather than the broader judgments with which those exceptions are not in accord.

To cite but one example, again in regard to Buddhism and by a better-informed layman than Lord Russell, Jerrold Schecter, writing in 1967, said:

> Buddhism in Asia is basic belief and bedrock identity; it influences power, sex, psychology and economics.

> Buddhism is not only religion and philosophy; it is also nationalism and ideology, it is the ultimate source of Asian values.
>
> . . . today in the Buddhist countries of Asia, the alms bowl has been overturned. The peaceful path of the Middle Way has been twisted into the new violence of street demonstrations with the blare of loudspeakers, the hollow crack of wooden clubs on skulls and the maddening fury of tear gas. Buddhism in Asia is a faith in flames.[4]

If this characterization by a journalist is correct about Buddhism at the beginning of the last third of the twentieth century, something of a drastic nature has happened in the past fifty years, or Max Weber was in error when he wrote that "to change the social order in this world neither early nor later Buddhism has attempted to do."[5] Careful reflection, I believe, will lead us to the conclusion that something of a drastic nature has happened in the past half century and, also, that Weber was not wholly correct in his sweeping generalization.

I submit two more random observations about religion in Asia before proceeding on to what I hope is a more structured approach to our concern. One is a statement by Wilfred Cantwell Smith in his *Islam in Modern History*. In discussing Pakistan as an Islamic state and the problem of modernity, he suggests that "one might almost argue that the fundamental religious problem for contemporary Muslims has to do with the fact that the impact of modernity upon the Islamic tradition has not been nearly strong enough."[6]

And, finally, Richard C. Bush, in his highly regarded paper "The impact of Communism on Religions in China," comes to the conclusion that the "result is a quiet, contained existence [of the religions] with little possibility for [their] growth or development."[7]

Now, what are we to do about the wide variety and frequent disparity of statements about our subject on the part of scholars and investigators and of indigenous participants whose opinions we respect? Obviously, we need to recognize what the disparity tells us, namely, that the situation is different in the instance of each religion, though there are analogous forces at work and, frequently, similar reactions to those forces. Further, in the instance of each religious area the standards for assessment and evaluation of the nature and degree of ferment vary as a result of the specific relationship of many factors, both historic and contemporary; also, the conditions to be assessed vary from area to area and from stratum to stratum within any one religious tradition. We need only to mention the differing norms and methods of approach employed by the investigator and the part they inevitably play in forming his particular conclusions.

Having in mind such complexities in treating the subject, I will focus attention upon India and Hinduism with the purpose of suggesting some aspects of religious ferment in that area and, perhaps, adumbrating also analogous situations in other religious areas of the Asian world.

One predominant and striking feature of the religious situation in many parts of Asia today is the expression in political forms of the idealized religious values of the past. From the proclamation if not the actualization of a Muslim state in Pakistan to the intense expression of Nichiren Japanese Buddhism in the form of Sōka Gakkai, traditional aspects of religious thought and practice are being brought before the public mind as constituting the ideal standards for personal and corporate life within the modern state.

In India and for Hinduism this has taken the form of what is perhaps best described as a conservative religious and cultural idealism, grounded in an idealized past. This idealism seeks to express itself meaningfully by entering into the political arena through a political party or arm that receives much of its strength from its ties to a so-called cultural organization that devotes its energies primarily to inculcating youth with a knowledge of and zeal for that past. The glorious past and its accomplishments are not only declared to be the proper standards for the present; they also furnish the divinely ordained key to the successful incorporation of modernity into the social structure and moral fiber of the contemporary nation-state. It is not the "modern"—whatever is meant by that term—that sets the norm and to which adjustment must be made. Rather, it is the traditional truth that gives the divine dharma, the cosmic law, to which all that is new or apparently different must be adjusted.

We are, of course, familiar with the Hindu renaissance and revival of the nineteenth century. One primary feature of that new self-consciousness was the conviction, closely associated with Swami Dayānand Saraswati and the Arya Samāj, that in the Vedas of early Aryan India are deposited the fundamental truths applicable to mankind at any time. The *Sanātanadharma*, the eternal religion, must be reinstituted among the Hindu-Indian people, and in that reinstitution will be their salvation, not only religiously but culturally, socially, and politically.

In the present century there have been a few principal groups that have built upon this conviction in various ways as they have attempted to bring their idealized religious values of the past into meaningful viability in the present. The Hindu Mahāsabhā and one of its early leaders, V. D. Savarkar, played an important part in putting forth an amalgam of traditional Hindu philosophy-theology, Indian-Hindu culture, and the custom morality associated with folk India and its traditions. Savarkar's *Hindutva*, or "Hinduness," was meant to convey all aspects of Hindu thought and ways of life as they were believed by him and his colleagues to have been followed in the days of India's glory. By placing emphasis upon what he held to be the property of all Indians in the twentieth century—namely, a common culture, a common history, a common classical language, a common country, and a common religion—Savarkar formalized the thought that has been at the foundation of the prominent examples of Hinduism in politics in India during recent decades. Hinduness includes all who are the natural-born inheritors of the seminal themes of classical Indian philosophy-theology; all who are surrounded by and participants in the broad, amorphous folk religion; and all who have received the cultural and social inheritance that distinguishes the Indian from other people. All who have received the gift of these values are bound together within the Hindu Sangathan. They are brothers within the Hindu community as a result of their Hinduness, which makes them unique among the world's peoples. And it is upon this basis, and this basis only, that the Hindu Rāshtra, the Hindu nation, can come into its own in the modern day.

Today two groups, one primarily cultural and the other political, are seeking by all possible means to rally the Indian people around the concept of Hinduness. One is the Rāshtriya Swayamsevak Sangh, or National Volunteer Organization, and the other is the Bhāratiya Jana Sangh, or Indian People's Party. The Rāshtriya Swayamsevak Sangh—or R.S.S., as it is commonly called—came into existence in 1925, calling itself a cultural organization with the purpose of training the Indian people in a philosophy of action founded upon their historical society and the cultural heritage of their traditional community. The Bhāratiya Jana Sangh—or Jana Sangh as it is usually called—is a product of the R.S.S., created in 1951 to be an expression of the R.S.S. in the political arena. In the past decade its rapid growth, particularly in the Hindi-speaking north, made it a force to be reckoned with, though, of course, given the current political situation in India, no one can tell just what its future will be.

The R.S.S. proclaims its firm conviction that there is an appropriate, in fact divinely, ordained foundation upon which Indian political policy and action must be based if India is to become the viable vehicle for Bharatiya Sanskriti and Dharma Rājya—that is, Indian Culture and the rule of spirituality. The cultural organization, the R.S.S., lays the basis for the political party, the Jana Sangh. Elements in one are noticeably present in the other, and the two intertwine until they become almost indistinguishable. Political action and Hindutva—Hindu religion, culture, and history—all become one and the same thing. To quote the leader of the R.S.S., Gurūji Golwalkar, "In Hindusthan, religion is an all absorbing entity. . . . it has become eternally woven into the life of the race, and forms, as it were, its very soul. With us every action in life, individual, social, or political, is a command of religion. . . . we are what our great religion has made us. Our race spirit is a child of our religion, and so with us culture is but a product of our all-comprehensive religion, a part of its body and not distinguishable from it."[8]

A study of Golwalkar's many speeches and writings reveals repeated emphasis on the basic tenets associated with the classical formulations of Hindu philosophy-theology; there is constant reiteration of the great tradition as it is presented by some of the present-day Hindu religious groups. The "eternal and ennobling values" that Golwalkar speaks of and that he is seeking to rejuvenate among the Indian people are fundamental themes recurring throughout Hindu literature. It is relatively simple to establish the close interweaving by Golwalkar and others of these ancient and still-appealing values with present-day India's concern to possess viable, indigenous moorings in the modern world.

These philosophical and religious tenets, together with idealized social forms that have supported them and that have also been sanctioned by them, are made the foundations for a religious-cultural-political rallying-together of the Indian-Hindu people. Non-Indian investigators, and many Hindus, may question the sincerity of or, perhaps more accurately, the way in which such groups and their leaders use these traditional religious concepts and stress their value—and those who doubt the political future and impact of these groups may be correct in their analysis. Nevertheless, there can be no doubt but that a primary aspect of the religious ferment in India today is expressing itself in a cultural-political form that gains its basic strength from a concentration upon idealized religious values that are maintained by the Mahasabha, the R.S.S., the Jana Sangh, and others to have flourished in the past.

A second feature of religious ferment to which I would draw attention focuses upon the norms of the social structure, the idealized ways of association and behavior, the custom moralities—those matters which in Hindu India generally have been considered to be a part of *Sanātanadharma*, the eternal truth by which men should live, in fact must live, if existence is to be proper and in accord with universal law. Following the injunction of W. Brede Kristensen that "every religion ought to be understood from its own standpoint, for that is how it is understood by its own adherents,"[9] it is essential that we recognize that for the mass of the adherents to Hinduism a central, if not the central, element of what they have understood to be religion is the manner in which life is lived through its daily associations, responsibilities, and pleasures.

The question for us is whether the various components so closely associated with traditional Hindu religion, especially at the popular folk level, are in ferment. Certainly we are aware that within the cities of India today there is an agitation, in some instances an almost chaotic excitement, that indicates more than mere superficial change. Associated as this ferment is with industrialization and massive populations gathered in settings that are very different from those of the traditional past, does this unfamiliar condition work toward, and perhaps demand, a change in the traditional norms of religious cult, social intercourse, and association? Does it affect the means whereby the established values of the religious past are conveyed to the present and future Hindu Indian?

And, of equal importance, what is the situation in regard to these matters in the villages and countryside that still contain the bulk of the Indian people? The ferment, it is true, is more readily apparent in the urban areas, but are we safe in concluding that the village and the countryside continue in their age-old ways without perceptible and meaningful change? I am certain that in this regard I do not need to cite the numerous studies of rural and village India that while recognizing the tendency of rural people to remain close to their traditional structures, also point out that the situation today is such that despite the hold of tradition upon them, the peoples of these areas are aware of the new opportunities that are confronting them. They are in many instances both aware of the opportunities and cautiously but with determination slowly setting about to become acquainted with that which is new.

In the matter of religious cult, we know that among some of the so-called modernized elite and others a process of cultic abbreviation is taking place.[10] But we know that the modern technology and resulting atmosphere that encourages such change also is furnishing means for the wider dissemination of the traditional values associated with and preserved by the ancient cultic forms. The few great temple complexes that in one form or another are associated with and are encouraging such supposedly modern and new things as hospitals and universities—such as at Tirupatti in southern India—despite the surface appearance of departing somewhat from the traditional, continue to educate the Hindu people in the purāṇic lore that is the core of popular Hinduism. Temples are being built and refurbished; loudspeakers, movie projectors, and printing presses are carrying the purāṇic and epic tales to the people of the villages and rural areas in a fashion reminiscent of the days when royal patronage of Hindu art and drama was the rule rather than the exception.

But we must be cautious here. The change is sometimes almost imperceptible. It can hardly be said that it is so intense that there is ferment. If we only listen to the voices of the intellectually elite whose modernization is almost but not quite exclusively a westernization—to those whom Professor Shils of Chicago described so well in his *The Intellectual between Tradition and Modernity: The Indian Situation*—we might easily come to the conclusion that Hindu cultic change is in reality the beginning of cultic disappearance. If we pay attention only, or primarily, to the words of leaders of certain modernized religious groups that are seeking to export Hinduism to the West as well as to revive Hinduism in India itself, we run the risk of making the false assumption that Hindu cult is fully cleansed of those aspects that the modernized Hindu considers to be unhealthy accretions to true Hindu worship. Whatever the case in regard to cult, ritual purity, religious-social rites of passage, and the like, we need to watch them carefully, knowing that much of the impact and persistence of Hinduism is to be found in them and their importance to the Indian people.

Only brief mention can be given to that most fascinating of subjects to the student of India—caste. The centrality of caste within the Indian social-religious structure, and in contemporary Indian politics also, is well recognized. Many studies by Indians and non-Indians alike dispute the conclusion of so many uninformed observers that caste is ceasing to play the central role in Indian life that it has in the past. Here if anywhere in Indian-Hindu social and religious life there is ferment. There is excitement and certainly there has been agitation. But rather than there being a disappearance of caste, as some Hindu apologists continue to claim, there is overwhelming evidence that caste is emerging, often in new forms, as one of the most decisive factors in Hindu life. This is not to suggest that caste as it actually is or as it is ideally formulated by some is evil. It is rather to insist that it is not inevitably crumbling before contemporary pressures. Lloyd and Susanne Rudolph, in their excellent study *The Modernity of Tradition*, put the situation very accurately when they wrote that in India "caste is losing the functions, norms, and structure once associated with it and acquiring new ones. It is serving the ritual and occupational goals of traditional society less, the mobility and participation goals of modern society more."[11]

For the religious tradition that is Hinduism, caste—whether in ancient form or in some newly emerging idealized guise—remains fundamental to the dharma that is incumbent upon the Hindu as it is normally understood. The ferment in regard to caste that has occurred during this century has been not only a movement of adaptability, though it has certainly been that; it has also resulted in a period of discovery in which both old and new functions of value to Hindu India have come to be recognized as being within the province of caste. Ferment has not meant disappearance of caste; rather, it has meant a reinvigoration of it, with the result that it is now venturing with confidence into new areas of operation.

The final aspect of religious ferment—or perhaps lack of it—that I would mention concerns the underlying intellectual affirmations, the inherited beliefs concerning the nature of being. For me these are best understood as the "visceral presuppositions or assumptions" that mark an individual and the others who with him constitute a religious-cultural tradition.

In his study *India As a Secular State*, Donald E. Smith begins by saying, "The religious temperament and outlook of the Indian people may have been exaggerated by some writers, but it is nonetheless true that religion has been the most powerful single factor in the development of Indian civilization."[12] The question that I would raise is, What is the present state of the traditional themes, the metaphysical formulations, upon which that religious temperament and outlook have been based?

If we consider the philosophy-theology—the various conceptions as to the nature of human and cosmic existence that have characterized Indian thought since the emergence of the Upanishads and the time of the Buddha and that constitute the core of the great tradition of Hinduism—it appears to be clear that these matters or beliefs are not considered by their intellectual inheritors to be inappropriate for the intelligent man and woman of today. With few exceptions, the Hindu intellectual, surrounded as he increasingly is by processes of modernization that appear to challenge so much of the traditional, makes his philosophic orientation fundamentally upon a base that is dependent upon themes and structures associated with the great thinkers of India's past—Shankara, Rāmānuja, Madhva, and others. In addition, he is the beneficiary of the Indian intellectual ferment of the past two centuries, with its renaissance of pride in things Indian and its attempt to reform and revive the tradition. As a result, the ancient philosophical and theological themes as interpreted by earlier thinkers are also made viable today because of the work of Ram Mohan Roy, Dayānand Saraswati, Vivekānanda, Radhakrishnan, and others. Today the Hindu intellectual proceeds from these basic themes to the consideration of the value or disvalue of new or foreign philosophic speculation. There are few Indian thinkers who set about to dispute the fundamental presuppositions that are the very warp and woof of the traditional Hindu *Weltanschauung*. Rather, the activity within Indian intellectual speculation (it can hardly be termed a ferment) is to be seen in the concern to demonstrate that the ancient themes, rightly understood, are supported by the rational norms and procedures associated with modernity. The end result is that the traditional core around which Indian-Hindu philosophy and religious speculation has revolved is held to be the *only* viable basis for a meaningful Hindu society in the modern present.

I have limited these last remarks to the Hindu intellectual and to the educated class in general. Of course, there are exceptions: there are some rebellious university-educated youth and there are business, political, and labor leaders at various levels for whom these cultural-religious moorings are outmoded vestiges of the past. But these are relatively few, and their not-very-frequent attacks upon the cherished metaphysical beliefs have so far resulted in little if any ferment.

At the wider level of the masses of the Hindu people the situation is similar. Here the awareness of the philosophical tradition is less precise, of course, yet the basic elements that the tradition is built upon and that the tradition perpetuates continue to be central to the life orientation of the Indian people. Dharma, Karma, Samsāra, Atman, Jiva, Ishvara, Avatāra—these and others under whatever local name—are the bedrock of Indian religion and common thought. Together with purāṇic legend, both local and nationwide, they give a religious quality and identity to Hindu life. The presence of ferment, of excitement, in regard to them is difficult to discover.

At the beginning of this essay I sought to make the obvious even more obvious by emphasizing the variety of assessments that can be made concerning religious ferment in Asia. I also stressed the role of the suggestive generalization as an aid to understanding, despite the dangers inherent in generalizations.

In the instance of India and Hinduism the generalization that observation forces upon me is that the religious ferment there, to the degree that it can be discovered, is one wherein the traditional is seeking to assert itself within the context of modernity. In so doing, it rejects the notion that modernity is something essentially contradictory to the core values of the tradition. These values are shruti—revelation from the Divine. They are founded in Ultimate Reality, and they are necessarily applicable to political life and forms and to social structures and relationships in any age.

If as students of Asia we ignore this fact in regard to any of the traditional religions of the area, however they formulate their basic themes, we run the grave danger of understanding them in our own terms rather than theirs. The Muslim of Pakistan and Indonesia, the Hindu of India, and the Buddhist of many areas of Asia will either continue to be extremely mysterious, or he will be assumed to be just like us, only perhaps not quite as modern. In either case he will remain unknown.

If this be true, then we will all too often see religious ferment where there is only momentary agitation without lasting significance; we will also run the risk of failing to discern the significant ferment that frequently, in a quiet fashion, renews the traditional while incorporating the new and modern into itself.

NOTES

1. Bertrand Russell, *The Autobiography of Bertrand Russell,* Vol. 2, *The Middle Years: 1914–1944* (New York, 1969), p. 191.

2. Mohammad Fadhel Jamali, *Letters on Islam* (London, 1965), p. 90.

3. R. N. Dandekar, "Hindu Intellectuals under Recent Impacts of Modern Culture," *Proceedings of the XI International Congress of the I.A.H.R.,* 1:90 (1968).

4. Jerrold Schecter, *The New Face of Buddha* (New York, 1967), p. xi.

5. Max Weber, *The Religion of India,* trans. H. H. Gerth and D. Martindale (New York, 1967), p. 227.

6. W. C. Smith, *Islam in Modern History* (Princeton, N.J., 1957), p. 225.

7. Richard C. Bush, 'The Impact of Communism on Religions in China," *Proceedings of the XI International Congress of the I.A.H.R.,* 3:72 (1968).

8. M. S. Golwalkar, *We: Or Our Nationhood Defined* (Nagpur, India, 1947), pp. 27 f. Quoted in J. A. Curran, Jr., *Militant Hinduism in Indian Politics: A Study of the R.S.S.* (New York, 1951), p. 29.

9. W. Brede Kristensen, *The Meaning of Religion* (The Hague, 1960), p. 6.

10. See Milton Singer, "The Great Tradition in a Metropolitan Center: Madras," in *Traditional India: Structure and Change* (Philadelphia, 1959).

11. Lloyd I. and Susanne Hoeber Rudolph, *The Modernity of Tradition: Political Development in India* (Chicago, 1967), p. 103.

12. Donald E. Smith, *India As a Secular State* (Princeton, N.J., 1963), p. vii.

2

Distillers of Fermentation

EDITORIAL NOTE

Selective Reception and Transmission As a Process of Religious Ferment

Robert J. Miller
University of Wisconsin

Analogy, though useful, leads one along treacherous paths of thought. Since we speak of ferment, it is natural to consider extension of the term and to attempt to draw an analogy between fermentation of grapes and fermentation of ideas in an individual mind. But such an analogy may lead us astray; we are, after all, dealing with a process occurring in a structure more comparable to an electronic device that is constructed to accept certain signals and to reject others—in short, the human ability to be selective. This ferment does not simply bubble around in a container—it is created or utilized or stopped in human minds by the presence of conflicting ideas, commitments to goals, and access to information.

Thus with the individuals considered in the chapters in this section. They are set to receive and transmit, perhaps in altered form, certain signals. From a possible range of alternative ideas that might have been chosen, they chose only a limited number. In electronic terms, their selectivity was high. Each person discussed in this section is, possibly, a unique case. Taken collectively, they suggest that religious ferment begins in an individual—or a group—with the triggering of a response to impinging noise, from which selection must be made. In our specific cases, the noise is in the form of Christian ethics or organizational models. In the more immediate present, as discussed by Bharati, the noise is internal but, in large part, traceable to prior and present external transmissions.

Access to information about many religious doctrines and organizational models is characteristic of the men discussed and of their contemporary parallels. From these available resources they select for retransmission only *particular* concepts, principles, or imperatives to action. As national and communal feelings become articulate in Asia, there is increasing emphasis on selection of signals from indigenous traditions for reinterpretation, followed by transmissions of new basic information after selective processing.

One of the distillers was a carrier of noise into an ongoing system. Sam Jordan, a Christian missionary to Iran, selected for transmission from Christian religious imperatives the emphases on work, dignity of labor, individual responsibility, equality of opportunity, and adherence to principle. These and other values derived from the social gospel he introduced into Iran as a hoped-for beginning of a fermentation process leading to changed attitudes and to moral uplift if not to conversion. Exhortation alone was not his only mode of transmission; action and exemplary behavior were also involved. It is significant that Jordan, like the subjects of other essays in this section (Keiu, Gandhi, Ch'oe, and contemporary Hindu reformists), reached into indigenous tradition for parallels and support for the ethic he promoted. In all these cases, selectivity by the distiller formed the basis for emergence of an eclectic doctrine. Such a doctrine, though sometimes far removed from a total and formal religious system, presupposed an audience tuned to receive the signals in a context of universal basic morality.

By the nineteenth century the ferment-stimulating signals that a Sam Jordan transmitted were being filtered through the minds of indigenous Asian intellectuals. Nakamura Keiu, M. K. Gandhi, and Ch'oe Che-u exemplify those who saw the path to national spiritual regeneration through change in the behavior of individuals. Each had sampled the wares of at least one religious tradition different from his own. While Keiu and Gandhi constructed models for action and transmission from ethical and religious concepts preselected by pious *secular* Christians, Ch'oe looked at the model that Christianity in China and Korea was transmitting, and then he directed his selective channels to reception of indigenous signals. Chong suggests, however, that even Ch'oe did not entirely tune out the noise of Christian signals.

For each individual discussed by our authors, religion was not an abstract. It was an imperative to action according to belief. Each asked for the translation of an idea, once received, into behavior. Gandhi and Ch'oe in some respects are the more modern in their eclecticism, in their selectivity, and in their attempts to reinterpret and retransmit Indian and Korean traditions. Both had access to the vast range of religious concepts from which they could draw elements to construct a new doctrine. Each translated his doctrine into a model for behavior and personally attempted to put it into practice. Each synthesized and simplified what he had taken from the various sources. Each led others to reexamine and reinterpret their own traditions, rather than to tune to external channels.

Bharati's essay, "The Language of Modern Hinduism," though utilizing other theoretical concepts, fits the electronic model sketched above. Instead of a single individual who is selecting and processing information for transmission, Bharati discusses the range of simplifiers, the modes of selectivity, and the actual media and technology employed by modern-day Hindu saints and religious modernizers. All attempt to spread an eclectic Hindu ethic, and the process evident in these attempts is not different in principle from that illustrated in previous papers. At one point, Bharati suggests that even the organizational prototypes and social actions that the reforming Hindu sects use are drawn in fact from models projected earlier by Christian missionaries.

Bharati prepares us for the next section, in which the signals, distilled, simplified, and selectively received (by an audience with less access to the originals in most cases), are reprocessed. They reverberate through organizations and societies, producing new religious ferment, and offer competing models of the good society.

Sam Jordan and the Evangelical Ethic in Iran

Yahya Armajani
Macalester College

During the summer of 1952 Iran was at the height of its struggle for the nationalization of its oil resources. The United Nations had virtually washed its hands of the affair, and the decision of the World Court in favor of Iran had not been effective. The British had confiscated oil tankers taking Persian crude oil to customers; and the United States, in order to pressure Iran to come to terms, had refused the loan that had been promised earlier. The Persian resentment of American intervention on the side of Great Britain had turned into anger and hatred. The Communist Tudeh party had a heyday in organizing anti-American demonstrations and rallies in Tehran and other parts of the country. The American Embassy had advised all United States citizens that it was more prudent to stay at home than to be seen in the streets. In the midst of all this turmoil, on June 21, 1952, news reached Tehran of the death of Dr. Samuel Martin Jordan, founder and president of Alborz College of Tehran and for forty-three years a missionary in Iran. A sorrowful hush fell over the people of Tehran. Almost instantly, all anti-American demonstrations ceased, and thousands thronged to the two memorial services held in his honor, which emphasized two aspects of Dr. Jordan's life—his services to the church and his contributions in the field of education in Iran.

In the huge outdoor memorial service held on the campus of the former Alborz College, over two thousand persons, among them former prime ministers and active leaders in every walk of life, had come to pay homage to this American who was unknown to his own countrymen. Of the dozen speakers on the platform, all but one were former students of Dr. Jordan's who were leaders in different phases of Persian national life. The only exception was the American ambassador, who was introduced by the chairman of the meeting, himself the head of the commission that had nationalized Iran's oil. Ambassador Henderson, who had never met Dr. Jordan, said that he had been "deeply impressed by the fact that although he [Jordan] ceased his labors in this country twelve years ago, his memory is still brightly green."[1]

The object of this great reverence and honor—Samuel Martin Jordan—was born in Stewartstown, Pennsylvania, on January 6, 1871. After entering Lafayette College in 1891, he decided to enter the ministry. His pastor wrote of him, "He has battled for himself all his way through academy, college and seminary. His vacations have almost without exception been spent in securing funds for his further course."[2]

Sam Jordan engaged heartily in college athletics and in 1894 became captain of one of Lafayette's most famous football teams. At Princeton Theological Seminary, where he began study in 1895, Jordan was influenced by the missionary impulse that had been an important part of "a New Protestantism which emphasized the individual rather than the system, which led to a release of energy much like that of the Reformation of the sixteenth century."[3] The American Board of Commissioners for Foreign Missions was organized in 1810. By the end of the nineteenth century the object of the missionary enterprise was the "evangelization of the world in one generation." Insofar as the bearers of the gospel were Americans, they were believers in the American experiment, were influenced by the implications of the American destiny, and were beneficiaries of the American way of life.

Perhaps no one articulated the imperialistic implications of the American destiny better than Senator Albert Beveridge of Indiana, who in 1900 said that God had

> not been preparing the English-speaking and Teutonic peoples for a thousand years for nothing. . . . He has made us the master organizers of the world. . . . He has given us the spirit of progress. . . . He has made us adepts in government. . . . And of all our race He has marked the American people as His chosen nation to finally lead in the regeneration of the world. This is the divine mission of America, and it holds for us all the profit, all the glory, all the happiness possible to man. We are trustees of the world's progress, guardians of its righteous peace.[4]

To be sure, most of the American missionaries were not interested in America's predominance in Asia nor in having their government take over control of other governments. But they were believers in the American way of life, which in their opinion was the direct result of the Christian gospel. They were interested in the salvation of individuals and in sharing the blessings with which the Lord had blessed America.

Inasmuch as the power and prestige of America were gifts of the Lord, the missionaries used them for the good of the cause. More than once they hoisted the American flag to save the innocent or used the prestige of the United States to gain special privileges for their schools and hospitals. When in 1903 the new American minister in Tehran, for reasons of his own, refused to receive the missionaries, the Reverend Lewis T. Esselstyn, secretary of the East Persia Mission, wrote a strong report to New York and objected to being treated at "arms length" by the minister, because "we cannot permit our work here to suffer by our being treated in this way . . . in a country where the rules of society are very important to our standing in the community."[5]

Samuel Jordan fell under the spell of the missionary movement and decided to go to the foreign field "as the place where one could do the most good to the greatest number the longest time." He applied to the Presbyterian Board of Foreign Missions on December 10, 1897, and was assigned to Tehran. He married Mary Wood Park on July 21, 1898, was ordained on August 30, and sailed with his bride for Iran on September 17. They arrived in Tehran on November 2, probably the last missionaries to travel by caravan over the Alborz Mountains from Rasht on the Caspian to Tehran. A few years later the Russians built a carriage road and established a system of post houses all along the route.

When the Jordans arrived in Tehran in 1898, the American Christian Mission in Iran was sixty-four years old. Since the missionaries had found the conversion of the Muslims in the Ottoman empire so difficult as to be almost impossible, they had developed the strategy of evangelizing the already existing Christians in the Middle East in the hope that they in turn would preach the gospel to their Muslim compatriots. On the basis of this plan, the American Board sent the Reverend Justin Perkins and Mrs. Perkins to Iran "to enable the Nestorian church through the grace of God, to exert a commanding influence in the spiritual regeneration of Asia."[6]

The American missionaries established evangelistic, educational, and medical work among the Nestorians in the province of Azarbāyjān, with their center in Urmia (now Rezā'iyeh). Partly because the missionaries realized that the Nestorians were not willing to evangelize the Muslims and partly because they discovered that the Persian Shi'is were more receptive than the Sunnis of the Ottoman empire, they decided to try working among the Muslims. So in 1870 the Mission to Nestorians was changed to the Mission to Persia, and two years later the Reverend James Bassett and Mrs. Bassett were transferred from Urmia to Tehran. Mr. Bassett's plan was "to avoid identification with one class. I wish, therefore, all our preaching to be in the Persian language, which Armenians, Jews & Mussulmans all understand."[7]

The conversion of the Persians did not prove easy, and the students in the Mission School during the first few years were Armenians, Jews, and Zoroastrians. Nevertheless, the Persians were polite enough to give the missionaries a hearing; and the Sufi influence, so prevalent among the Shi'i clergy, made them easier to get along with than their Sunni counterparts. As early as 1900 a missionary was allowed to preach in the bazaar of the shrine city of Qom, south of Tehran, where he had friendly conversations with a number of the clergy. A year later this same missionary, Mr. Esselstyn, in company with Samuel Jordan, was actually invited by Hāji Molla Ali, the Mojtahed of the region, to attend Friday prayers in the chief mosque in Semnan, a town on the road to Mashhad. After prayers, Mr. Esselstyn was invited to preach. He ascended the pulpit and "offered prayer in the name of Christ, and ascribing praise to the Trinity." Then he preached a sermon on repentance. When he descended from the pulpit, the Hāji said, "Praise God for the good teaching you gave these people. I am very thankful to you."[8]

The number of conversions made among the Muslims in Iran is nothing compared to missionary successes in India and East Asia, but compared to the rest of the Muslim world it is considerable. The fact that a small Persian-speaking church has been established, that a man with the definite Muslim name of Mahmud was the leading evangelist in Tehran until his death a short while ago, that another named Ali is the former head of the Bible Society, and that the Anglican Bishop for Iran is none other than the Right Reverend Hasan Dehqani-Tafti—all testify to the relative success of the missionaries.

Nevertheless, it was not through conversion that the American missionaries influenced the people of Iran, but rather through the application of the Christian ethic. The missionaries were the harbingers of change. It was their deepest desire to change the country by conversion, but realizing the impossibility of that, they were happy to change the attitude of the young through education and to introduce new values. The sum total of these values is what is meant by the evangelical ethic; and Samuel Jordan, who took charge of an elementary school in 1900 and built it to a college by 1930, did more than anyone to teach it to the Persians. A few Persians who had been in contact with the West had some inkling of Western values, but in the person of Jordan and his school they saw the embodiment of the very change they desired for their country. It was often heard in the provinces that "up in Tehran the Americans have a factory which makes men."

The evangelical or Protestant or Christian ethic was made up of at least three ingredients. One was piety, which comprised bans on smoking, swearing, drinking, and breaking of the Sabbath. The second was a set of values such as the dignity of labor, the virtue of service, the equality of women, the importance of the individual, and love of one's country. The third was democracy, which included equality of men and of opportunity, initiative, and perhaps free enterprise. All of this was gift-wrapped in an American system of education. Most Persians who came under its influence accepted it as a panacea for the ills of the country.

In all mission schools everywhere, and certainly in the ones in Iran, piety was enforced universally. Students were not allowed to smoke. A cigarette was defined as a "useless tube at one end of which is fire and the other end a fool." Any student caught smoking would be fined the cost of one month's supply of cigarettes, and the money would be used for winter fuel.[9]

Observance of Sunday was uncontested when most of the students were Christians or Jews. When Muslim students gained the majority, the Persian government in 1913 asked the mission schools to close on Friday and to conduct school on Sunday. This was not acceptable to the missionaries, and after long negotiations it was agreed to close both on Fridays and on Sundays; the results of the new arrangement were better than anticipated.

Perhaps the ban on swearing was hardest for the Persian student to get adjusted to, for ordinary conversation in the Middle East is punctuated by appealing to the Imams, the Prophets, and Allah. Somehow the Biblical admonition not to take the name of the Lord in vain was not interpreted by the Muslims in the same way as by the Christians. It was hard to refrain, and the school seemed to be full of reporters. At every infraction the student's mouth would be sprayed with quinine. The missionaries were no doubt hitting two birds with one stone, guarding the student against the ever-present malaria and curing him of the habit of using the name of God in ordinary conversations.

The matter of drinking remained an embarrassment to the missionaries in the Muslim countries. Drinking was known among the Muslims to be a "Christian habit." Mr. Bassett wrote in 1890 that "all non-Mohammedans are in the habit of drinking wine or arak, usually both . . . they think it no sin to drink."[10] Most of the taverns were owned by Armenians and were frequented by Muslims. In the early 1920's a Muslim clergyman asked Dr. Jordan to forbid his "coreligionists" (that is, Armenians) to sell drinks and ask them to choose some other business. Dr. Jordan is reported to have replied, "In our religion drinking is not forbidden, but we missionaries don't drink. But in your religion drinking is forbidden. You order the Muslims not to buy drinks and the Armenians will be out of business."[11] Apparently not all missionaries agreed with Jordan that in Christianity drinking was not forbidden, and they tried in every way to rout out drinking among both the Christians and the Muslims.

In his attempt to "shut up the whisky business in Tehran," Mr. Esselstyn in cooperation with the chief Mojtahed of Tehran persuaded the Shah to issue a decree to close all the taverns. The Shah issued the royal farman on the religious authority of the chief Mojtahed and the "American Christian priest Esselstyn." In his report to the board in New York, Mr. Esselstyn expressed surprise that his name was mentioned, but "they all know I was at the bottom of it all right . . . in a few days we will have things in such shape, D. V. that a man can't get a drink of anything to make him drunk at a shop."[12]

Piety, however, was not among the important contributions of the Christian missionaries. The most important aims, aside from individual conversion, was the building of character by inculcating Christian values. Education was the means, and the missionaries established schools wherever they went. In going over a mass of letters and reports, one is impressed with a sharp difference of opinion between the evangelistic missionaries, who considered the schools as means of conversion, and the educational missionaries, who wanted to prepare the students "for a life of usefulness."[13]

In 1906 an evangelistic missionary gave his reason for supporting schools: "We are put here to fight Mohammedanism; schools and hospitals are our guns."[14] In the same year Samuel Jordan, as though in rebuttal, explained why he wanted schools:

> The young oriental educated in Western lands as a rule gets out of touch with his home country. He looses sympathy with his own people. Too often he discards indiscriminately the good and the bad of the old civilization and fails to assimilate the best of the West. He loses all faith in his old religion and gets nothing in its stead. . . . in mission schools and colleges we adapt the best Western methods to the needs of the country. While we retain all that is good in their own civilization, we also inspire their students with enthusiasm for the high ideals and the pure standards of Christian lands.[15]

Not only were the missionaries eager to open schools, but the Persian modernists were equally eager to attend them so that they might establish a closer contact with the West. The peculiar political situation of Iran as a buffer state between the rival imperialisms of Great Britain and Russia made it expedient for the Persians to involve a neutral third power. The United States was the best candidate. Even though the British, French, Germans, and Russians had all opened schools in Iran, it was the American School in Tehran to which leaders of the country, including the royal family, sent their sons. Since the American School had the only dormitory facilities in the country, the sons of tribal chieftains and the intellegentsia from the provinces came to Dr. Jordan to be educated.

Habl ul- Matin, the liberal Persian newspaper published in Calcutta, in a 1907 article criticized the foreigners employed by the Persian government and advised that they be replaced by Americans for the following reasons: "Ninety percent of Japanese progress has been caused by employing Americans. America is a republic which means that individual Americans are not agents of their government. They are rich and don't need our wealth. They are progressive and they are helpful." To Dr. Jordan the above lines meant that America had "a mission in the world of civilization, benevolence and helpfulness."[16]

Character-building was the most important business of education, and one of the ingredients of a good character was the willingness to work. This was precisely what was needed in the modernization of Iran. To the Persians, as to the rest of the Asians, manual labor was degrading. The nobility and the educated never worked with their hands, and it was the highest goal of a Persian to be educated so that he would not need to dirty his hands. In the early days most Persian students went to school with a servant carrying each one's books. Perhaps Dr. Jordan's love of athletics induced him to approach the subject of work by teaching the Persians to play. Even this was not easy, for the Persian young men, with their cloaks and loose-fitting shoes, were not dressed for playing. At recess time they would sedately promenade up and down the walks and carry on polite conversation. Jordan had to induce the students to take off their hats and long coats and throw a ball around. In 1910 he started a summer camp in the nearby mountains. The students wore scout uniforms, and every afternoon they engaged in games, hiking, planting trees, and other activities that were considered "undignified" for an educated man. In 1914 many a noble eyebrow was raised when the Persians heard that Dr. Jordan and twenty of his students had climbed 19,000-foot-high Mount Damavand, located fifty miles northeast of Tehran. Gradually, games such as soccer, basketball, and tennis were introduced, and intramural competitions were added to interschool ones in track as well as team sports.

In 1915 Samuel Jordan was able to buy forty-four acres of land outside the north wall of the city for a college campus. The problem of teaching the dignity of labor was still on his mind one day in about 1917 when he saw a mule loaded with shovels. It occurred to him that they were the ideal thing for clearing off the ground for a soccer field. He bought the whole load. Then he called the upperclassmen together and said to them: "You know we have bought land for a new campus. We need a football field. Here is the way to get it." Then he threw a shovel over his shoulder and walked toward the new campus, and the students followed suit. This is the story in his own words:

> We marched out through the principal avenues of Tehran, past the home of the Prime Minister and other grandees, and those boys were having the time of their lives. They perfectly realized that they were enacting a declaration of independence. They were outraging all the conventions and proprieties of Iran and they were not afraid for they were headed by the president of the college. We put in several hours of good stiff work. At the end I said, "I trust you realize what you have done. I want it to go down in the history of the college that the first work on the new campus was not done by peasants receiving twenty cents a day for their labor but by the self-respecting students of the college who wished to show by action as well as by words that a New Era had come to Iran and henceforth any kind of work that is of service to mankind is honorable."[17]

That example was followed in succeeding years. The students not only leveled soccer fields but built roads and planted trees and removed dirt. Later, work scholarships were introduced and students held responsible jobs in all departments of the college. The initial letters of American College of Tehran spelled ACT, and this became the motto of the college. Later, in the Persianization of foreign names, "American" was replaced by "Alborz," partly so that ACT would still remain the motto. The cry everywhere on the campus was, "Don't just sit there, do something." Every college student memorized the English poem:

> Try, try, try again
> It is a lesson you should heed,
> If at first you don't succeed
> Try, try, try again.[18]

Alongside the dignity of labor, the evangelical ethic included service to others without personal gain. Until the third decade of the twentieth century Iran underwent numerous famines and epidemics, during which thousands perished. During the epidemics of 1853, 1861, 1866, 1871, and 1904 the missionaries gave unstintingly of their service and of their lives. In the great famine of 1917–1918, which gripped the whole country, the missionaries, as usual, set up relief work. Dr. Jordan challenged the members of the senior class to volunteer their services. They accepted the challenge, made a social survey of the city, and manned the relief centers. It is estimated that they fed over fifty thousand persons. That sons of the privileged, instead of escaping famine and disease, would plunge themselves into the fray and fight it made a great impression in the country.

From then on, students took part in social service, went to the villages to help teach sanitation, and volunteered to take part in literacy programs. In a school song, the students sang, "Our aim is love and service of mankind."

Wherever the missionaries went, they preached the equality of men and women. In most countries they were the first to open schools for women and to bring professional women teachers, doctors, and nurses as examples to show that women could perform such tasks. In 1889, when the first missionary female physician, Dr. Mary Smith, arrived in Tehran, scores went to stare at her and to find out how it was "possible for a woman to have enough knowledge to be a doctor." Shortly afterward, when Naser al-Din Shah visited the girls' school in Tehran, he asked to see the woman doctor and wanted her to feel his pulse and tell him the state of his health.[19] In 1904, however, Mozaffar al-Din Shah was persuaded to issue a decree forbidding Muslim girls to go to the mission school, where they were "taught to wear high shoes and long skirts."[20] But such decrees could not stop the tide of progress.

The contributions of the missionaries in the advancement of the women of Iran are undeniable. Early in their careers the Jordans decided that it was not enough to teach women, but that it was equally important to teach the men to accept educated women; so Mrs. Jordan joined her husband in educating men. In 1915, when Arthur Boyce went to Iran on a permanent basis as the vice-president of the college, his wife, Ann Stocking Boyce, who had herself been teaching in the girls' school, became a teacher of men. Many a father was seen shaking his head, wondering if he had done the right thing in letting his son be taught by a woman.

Mrs. Boyce, who taught in both the boys' and girls' schools, was the founder of the magazine *Alam-e Nesvān* (World of Women), which for twelve years was the leading (sometimes the only) Iranian magazine devoted to the uplift of women. In any study of the progress of women in Iran it is essential to study the pages of the *World of Women*.

Mrs. Jordan was a dedicated teacher, and generations of

students who passed under her instruction believe that she was among the best teachers of English as a foreign language. But she was also a feminist. Almost every one of her students memorized the statement "No country rises higher than the level of the women of that country," and practically every student had to write a composition on the subject.

Important ingredients of the evangelical ethic were democracy, freedom of the individual, and the equality of men. Samuel Jordan was a close observer of the Persian revolution. In 1909 he wrote: "Old Persia is a thing of the past. . . . Persia will never return to the days of her despotism and darkness . . . we are at the opening of a new era and the time is ripe for a forward movement in our educational work."[21] In the school, Muslims, Christians, Jews, and Zoroastrians studied and played together as equals.

Nowhere was this spirit of equality more manifest than among the resident students. In the dining hall the students took turns at serving the tables. It was quite a sight to see a prince or a son of the prime minister serve food to a student who was so poor that he was on full scholarship.

In 1907, when there was a student demonstration at the school instigated by a young *sayyed* (descendant of the Prophet), the mission station, in Jordan's absence, decided not to admit *sayyeds* or other Muslims that wore turbans. To Jordan this was class distinction. He interpreted the demonstration as "due in great part to political change taking place here. The pupils had become imbued with the spirit of liberty and the idea that the governed should have a voice in the government so they proposed to have a voice in the management of the school."[22]

Special classes were conducted in parliamentary government, societies were organized, and students translated *Robert's Rules of Order,* which became popular among the actual practitioners of democracy in the Persian Majles (Parliament). The students were encouraged to publish a newspaper of their own, the only one of its kind in the whole country.

Samuel Jordan and his colleagues also strengthened the sense of nationalism among the Persians. As early as 1902 he bemoaned the fact that "the better class of young Moslems are utterly lacking in patriotism."[23] Even though he thought that the West had a great deal to contribute, he did not want the

Persians to be a nation of imitators. So he extolled the good points of Persian civilization as few Persians did.

In an article for the Persian-language newspaper *Ra'd*, Jordan wrote: "The progress of any country depends upon the willingness of its citizens to sacrifice. . . . What the Persians have not realized is that patriotism is not just bravery in the battlefield but the daily hard work and the unsung services to the people of the country."[24] The school had literary societies to investigate the riches of Persian literature for the uplift of the country and dramatic clubs to depict the glories of the past. The four houses into which the students were divided for intramural purposes were named after Persian heroes. At a time when the majority of Persians were imitating Western architecture, Jordan insisted that the buildings of the college be Sasanian on the outside and that they display American efficiency on the inside. School songs popularized the nobility of work and the love of country more than anything else. Under the direction of Mrs. Jordan, each graduating class wrote a song; these were sung every day in the assembly and also by the youth outside.

This same nationalism proved to be the college's undoing. The time came when Persian nationalism would not permit foreigners to run its educational institutions. In 1940, on the eve of Dr. Jordan's seventieth birthday, the college, along with all other foreign schools, was taken over by the government. Reza Shah Pahlavi sent Dr. Jordan a message assuring him "that there was no ill feeling or criticism of the American schools, only great appreciation and gratitude for all that they had done for Iran, but the government had adopted the policy that henceforth all schools should be wholly under the control of the government."[25]

After the war Dr. Jordan went back to Iran for what turned out to be a triumphal visit. At a reception the minister of court of the new, young Shah gave a speech, expressing the hope that the Americans would reestablish Alborz College. But the Presbyterian Board was not interested. The hope, however, has not died and is still expressed from time to time.

Jordan was in the habit of calling his program a "constructive revolution." The Persians liked what he had to offer. In addition to decorations given to him by the Persian government, there are now in Tehran a Jordan Hall, a Jordan School, a Jordan Library, and a Jordan Boulevard. As though these were not enough, on the eve of his seventy-seventh birthday, his admirers unveiled an alabaster bust of Dr. Jordan in Tehran. So far as I know, this is the only statue erected by public subscription in honor of a foreigner in all of the Middle East.

Generally speaking, the history of Iran in the past century and a half has been the story of the reaction of its people to Western civilization. Even though they rejected the imperialism of the West, they were fascinated with its technology and accepted it wholeheartedly. On all other matters dealing with values and institutions they have been ambivalent. The history of Iran, however, has been long enough and the experience of the Persians with other cultures has been deep enough to show that pure technology within the framework of existing institutions would not bring desired results. It is necessary to create the institutions, values, and atmosphere that created the technology of the West in the first place.

The missionaries were the bearers of these values, which were reputedly the products of the Judeo-Christian and Greco-Roman traditions, molded by the Renaissance, the Reformation, the Enlightenment, and a few political and technological revolutions. The values of the dignity of labor, the virtue of service, equality of women, the importance of the individual, love of one's country, democracy, and initiative were among the best fruits of Western civilization. The Persians were attracted by them.

The question remains and is being argued whether it is possible to use the values of the West without going through the experiences that produced them. There are those who maintain that Iran must go through the experiences of the West in order to create the values of the West. This is not the place to argue the point. But even if this were true, the Persians in their long history have had more than one renaissance and reformation. Furthermore, pre-Islamic Iran was not too distant from the Greeks, nor is Islam so different from Christianity, that Persians could not graft these values onto their own heritage. The point is that the Persians seem to be trying.

Even though the American mission schools have been closed for thirty years, graduates of them still meet. The women support a clinic in Tehran and donate hours in voluntary social service. When the American missionaries showed a willingness to enter the field of education again, the Persians raised three hundred thousand dollars to match a similar gift from the United States, the Persian government donated land in the suburbs of Tehran, and Damavand College was opened, teaching the same values taught by Dr. Jordan.

NOTES

1. Arthur C. Boyce, *Alborz College of Tehran and Dr. Samuel Martin Jordan, Founder and President,* mimeographed for limited use, p. 50.

2. Persia Mission Files, Presbyterian Historical Society, MS. J. 766.

3. James A. Field, Jr., *America and the Mediterranean World, 1776–1882* (Princeton, N.J., 1969), p. 69.

4. Congressional Record, 56th Congress, 1st sess., p. 711.

5. East Persia Mission Microfilm, Presbyterian Historical Society (hereafter referred to as Microfilms), Vol. 186, No. 15 (1903).

6. *A Century of Mission Work in Iran, 1834–1934* (Beirut, n.d.), p. 2.

7. *Ibid.*, p. 26. For a full account of missionary work in Tehran see James Bassett, *Persia: Eastern Mission* (Philadelphia, 1890).

8. Microfilms, Vol. 183, No. 10.

9. Shokrollah Naser, *Ravesh-e Dr. Jordan* (Tehran, 1945), p. 17.

10. Bassett, *Persia*, p. 117.

11. Naser, *Ravesh-e Dr. Jordan*, p. 13.

12. Microfilms, Vol. 184, No. 13.

13. Microfilms, Vol. 186, No. 26.

14. Microfilms, Vol. 189, No. 1.

15. Microfilms, Vol. 189, No. 2.

16. Microfilms, Vol. 190, No. 45.

17. Boyce, *Alborz College*, p. 30.

18. Naser, *Ravesh-e Dr. Jordan*, p. 53.

19. *A Century of Mission Work in Iran*, p. 53.

20. *Ibid.*, p. 87.

21. Microfilms, Vol. 192, No. 22.

22. Microfilms, Vol. 190, Nos. 25 and 28.

23. Naser, *Ravesh-e Dr. Jordan*, attached to p. 16.

24. *Ibid.*

25. Boyce, *Alborz College*, p. 40.

Nakamura Keiu: The Evangelical Ethic in Japan

Jerry K. Fisher
Macalester College

"Can a nation be born at once?" This question was posed in 1876 by William Elliot Griffis in his introduction to *The Mikado's Empire.*[1] Ninety years later, scholars are still amazed that Japan seems to have passed through precisely that experience. In a little more than a decade, loosely knit feudal alliances were transformed into a powerful central government; class distinctions, which were so important to the maintenance of social and political harmony in Tokugawa Japan, were officially abolished; a national, compulsory educational system was established; and the economy had become both national and international.

Griffis answered his own question by relying on the evangelical dictum: "With God all things are possible."[2] Few modern scholars are willing to leave anything to God, and in recent years it has become popular to stress the continuity between the Tokugawa and the Meiji eras as a partial explanation of Japan's amazing feat. This new scholarship maintains that much of what seemed to be a miraculous transformation was actually the culmination of processes begun well before Commodore Perry steamed into Edo Bay. We have had studies in Tokugawa education, Tokugawa religion, Tokugawa economy, and even in Tokugawa polity that help support this view. It has also been shown conclusively that many of the new leaders of the Meiji period were lower samurai who began their climb during the feudal era.

But whether change in the first decade of the Meiji Period was miraculous or the culmination of processes begun during the Tokugawa era, it was, nonetheless, extremely rapid—much too rapid for certain elements of Japanese society. In some *han*, feudal loyalties within the peasantry were so strong that spontaneous resistance to centralized political structures attracted tens of thousands of followers. Furthermore, once central control was established, they benefited little from the new structures, which taxed them more efficiently and compelled their able-bodied children to attend public schools and to serve in a conscript army. Nor were samurai immune to adjustment problems; many squandered their pensions and fell to the depths of poverty. There was one group, however, which was surprisingly resilient during the turmoil of the early Meiji era: the samurai intellectuals. Although there were men like Saigō Takemori, who found himself leading a revolt against the new order, there was surprisingly little alienation among samurai intellectuals, who were both the products of the Tokugawa and creatures of the Meiji. This study proposes to investigate one aspect of that phenomenon.

There were at least three possible reasons why the Tokugawa-Meiji samurai intellectual was able to adjust to the new environment with little discernible malaise. First of all, the structures of early Meiji society were such that most intellectuals could achieve their life goals through participation in society. There was room in Meiji Japan for a Fukuzawa Yukichi, a Niijima Jo, and even an intransigent conservative Confucian scholar like Motoda Eifu. The door to success was wide open for the intelligent samurai—at least during the first years of the Meiji era. It was the age in which Takahashi Korekiyo, a future prime minister, could return from the United States in 1868, where he had been an indentured servant, and proceed to amass and squander several small fortunes while moving rapidly back and forth from one job to another: as teacher, translator, stipended student, and in and out of no less than three government ministries—all before he reached the age of thirty.[3] By 1874 Fukuzawa Yukichi complained that a mediocre scholar of Western learning who invested a meager one hundred yen and three years of his time to study Western languages could command a salary of fifty to seventy yen per month: a rate of profit, he claimed, that not even a usurer could match.[4]

A second explanation for why there seemed to be little alienation among Tokugawa-Meiji intellectuals is that their values had been transformed so that they could achieve their goals even in the new Meiji government. This position maintains that Fukuzawa Yukichi and many of his Meirokusha colleagues were modern, emancipated men who introduced Western thought to Japan because they had rejected their Tokugawa heritage. The continuity between the Tokugawa and Meiji eras was the individual himself. The process of change between the eras took place in the mind of each intellectual. There is, however, a third possibility, which has not been sufficiently explored. In this essay, I shall endeavor to show that one of the reasons "a nation could be born at once" and still leave few of its intellectuals frustrated aliens in their own land was because many intellectuals with a good, late Tokugawa Confucian upbringing felt very much at home in Meiji Japan. They were not only comfortable in the new, modern Meiji world, but they contributed greatly to its establishment and to its perpetuation.

The subject of this exposition is Nakamura Keiu, one of the most prominent of the Tokugawa-Meiji intellectuals. Nakamura was born in Edo in 1832. Before he was a year old, rice riots by destitute poor had penetrated into the great cities—even into the seat of the Tokugawa government. When Keiu was six years old, Ōshio Heihachirō, a samurai Confucian scholar serving the Tokugawa *bakufu*, led an uprising of peasants and townsmen in Osaka which left much of the city in shambles. As a youth, Nakamura lived through some of the most turbulent years in Japanese history. The samurai class, of which he was a member, was heavily in debt to the merchants; the Tokugawa government, to which his family owed their allegiance, was in an advanced state of decay; and the nation itself faced the possibility of being torn apart by the Western powers.

As Nakamura rapidly ascended the ranks as a student and then teacher at the Shōheikō, the official Tokugawa Confucian school, he was not unmindful of the world about him. He began to study the Dutch language when he was sixteen—six years before Perry's visit to Japan. By 1855 he was trying to learn English and was beginning to have grave doubts about the wisdom of the Tokugawa policy. A recently discovered document tells us much about Nakamura's thinking in the late 1850's. In that essay, entitled "Treatise on Western Learning," Nakamura stated that it was necessary for the Japanese to pursue Western studies. He also maintained that it was absolutely essential that Western studies be approached in the correct manner. He explained this by saying:

> In order to understand this new field of knowledge, we must dwell within its midst. We must become fully acquainted with some aspect of it in order to grasp its

essence. The sage does not forget this point. Look at it this way, presume everything in the land is dried out. However, within this drought-wrought land there is water. There is water in the sea, there is water in the river—we could carry it from there. But if we dig a well in the dried earth, water can also be obtained—it will spring forth to nourish the land. Western "skills" are not just clever tricks or stunts that can be simply mastered. Their ultimate source lies in the same intellectual stream as our own.[5]

Nakamura was approaching the problem of understanding the West with tools he had developed as a Confucian scholar: grasp the essence, do not become entangled with nonessential elements. When, in 1866, he had an opportunity to go to England to observe the West at first hand, he took it.

Victorian England presented Nakamura with a thoroughly understandable model. He began to realize that Christianity was at the center of Western culture and that if one did not understand how it affected the morals and practices of the people, then one could never understand the *products* of Western civilization. Nakamura was away from Japan just fifteen months, but he brought home an *omiage*, a souvenir which he felt captured the driving spirit behind the West's position of strength in the world: Samuel Smiles's most successful publication, *Self Help*. Interlacing moral dicta with biographical examples, Smiles bombarded his readers with Victorian evangelical values. Smiles endeavored to answer the question: "Why is England the greatest nation in the world?" And in publications such as *Self Help*, he showed that England was great because so many of its people were superior; its people were superior because they were good Christians. In Smiles's mind, Christianity was the source of England's power, and its "essential characteristics" were "the virtues of constancy, energy, perseverance, industry, patience, accuracy, cheerfulness, hope, self-denial, self-culture, self-respect, power of good example, [and] nobility of character."[6]

This was precisely the medicine that Japan needed for her sickness, thought Nakamura, because the Japanese people were, at that time, the antithesis of Smiles's ideal. In an article published in February 1875 entitled "Thesis on Changing the Character of the Japanese People," Nakamura's view of the waywardness of his countrymen can be clearly seen. He wrote: "[The Japanese] still indulge in wine and women as they always have. . . . They do not know the way of heaven—they have no morals. They pay no attention to their work nor do they realize the necessity to work diligently. . . . They do not like to study nor endure difficulties. They have no perseverance."[7]

Self Help made its first Japanese appearance in March 1871 under the title *Saikoku risshi hen*, which can be translated "How the West Succeeds." The popularity of the book was phenomenal, and Japanese scholars have since called it "The Bible of the Meiji era." Since that first Japanese translation, *Self Help* has been in print almost continuously.[8] The book did quite well in the West, too, 250,000 copies having been sold by the turn of the century.[9] In 1872 Nakamura published another Meiji-era classic, a translation of John Stuart Mill's *On Liberty*.

A close examination of both Nakamura's and Smiles's ideas elicits interesting comparisons. A basic tenet of Confucian ethics is that men, not institutions, determine the course of history. In his writings, Nakamura constantly pressed this point. There was little wonder that he was immediately attracted to Smiles. So central to Smiles was this concept that he began his famous *Self Help* with the following quotations:

> The worth of a State, in the long run, is the worth of the individuals composing it.—J. S. Mill

> We put too much faith in systems, and look too little to men.—B. Disraeli[10]

Compare these statements with those made in Meiji 8 (1875) by Nakamura Keiu:

> Government is like a cup which holds water: the people are like the water in the cup . . . if we change the shape of the container, the water which fills it has no change in character whatsoever. More important than changing the government is to change the character of the people. If day by day we can get rid of their soiled old ways and their character becomes fresh and new, we have hope.[11]

In the waning years of the Tokugawa *bakufu*, Nakamura Keiu had advocated digging a well to tap the ultimate source of all knowledge. By 1875 he felt that the government had located that source, but only if its nourishing waters were used would the Japanese people be saved.

However, there was hope! The Confucian and the evangelical ethics both emphatically stated that man could be saved. While the preacher waxed eloquent about sin and repentance, Smiles, the Victorian social practitioner, found the road to salvation to be the same as Nakamura did: all men must be taught how to live as men *should* live; education, especially moral education, was the means toward this end.

In order to teach others, one must be upright himself. For Nakamura, this was no obstacle, for evangelical prohibitions and commandments seem to have appealed to him even as a young man. The following are a list of dicta Keiu drew up for himself when he was twenty-two years old, well before he had come into contact with Western ideas:

1. Don't forget the virtues of loyalty and filial piety.
2. Don't forget the importance of correct bearing in all of your actions.
3. Don't use untrue words—neither lie nor exaggerate.
4. Cut away sexual desire—this is especially important for young people.
5. Study everything and don't be lazy.
6. Don't start reading a Dutch book and not finish it.
7. In all things criticize yourself but don't criticize others.
8. Cut off bad thoughts.
9. Be of sincere mind—don't be superficial or indulge in hypocrisy.
10. Always keep your blessings in mind, be grateful to your mother and father, don't forget the toils of the farmers, don't be lazy about anything you do.[12]

Nakamura Keiu's biographers tell us that the above credo is indicative of the way he thought and acted throughout his life.[13] But his intellectual endeavors did not stop with Smiles's type of teachings and actions. In fact, Nakamura's thought did not even begin with evangelical strictures: it began with Neo-Confucian ethics and metaphysics. At the Shōheikō, Nakamura came under the influence of Sato Issai, one of the leading scholars of the Ōyōmei school of Neo-Confucianism in nineteenth-century Japan.[14] The Ōyōmei school followed the teachings of the Chinese sage Wang Yang Ming (1472–1524), a monist who viewed the universe as a collection of essences each metaphysically complete in itself. Thus, for Ōyōmei, men existed as individuals, full, complete unto themselves. Feudal hierarchies had no logical place in Ōyōmei thought, nor was society held together by family ties or the class ethics of the samurai. It is true that Nakamura mentioned the importance of loyalty and filial piety in his credo, but in the context of the entire statement, they were certainly not central to the ethics enunciated. Loyalty appeared to be more important as a personal discipline than as a system of behavior. Filial piety was defined by Nakamura not in terms of duty but in terms of thanksgiving; one was grateful to one's parents just as one was thankful to the farmers who worked hard to produce the food that one ate. In later writings, Nakamura's gratitude to his parents could be described best by the concept "love."[15]

The personal ethics articulated by Nakamura focused on the cardinal sin of evangelical Christianity: indolence. He assumed that man knew what he must do (and must not do); the only problem involved was putting his knowledge into action. But how did man know what to do? Nakamura spoke to this question in a work entitled "A Treatise on the Oneness of Morals and Happiness."[16] In this essay, Nakamura took a traditional Confucian concept, *tendō* (the way of heaven), approached it as an Ōyōmei scholar, and equated it with a Christian concept of the Laws of God *(rosu obu goddo)*. The metaphysics is taken from Wang Yang Ming. *Ten* (heaven) was not something that was external to man; it was not above, below, or around him; it dwelt within him. To follow the Way of Heaven was thus a natural act on the part of man: it was to obey the commandment written upon his heart. Ōyōmei monism did not isolate each individual. Each individual was complete but was of the same essence as other individuals; thus a major thrust of this philosophy was universality.[17]

Had Samuel Smiles been able to understand Nakamura's theology, it is unlikely that he would have agreed that they were talking about the same thing. But Nakamura knew precisely how Victorian ethics supported his Confucian world view. The ethics of both Smiles and Nakamura assume a static and constant ethical standard. The laws of God were indelibly written on man's conscience. If Smiles had been true to his Calvinist heritage, he might have questioned whether or not only the saved were capable of knowing God's will; but Nakamura, the

Confucian scholar, had no doubts about this matter: *all men* had a natural capacity to follow the Way of Heaven, and Nakamura's Way of Heaven was the same for all men! The concept of original sin was alien to him, but Nakamura felt that Smiles's teachings were applicable to all men and were particularly well suited to Japan's needs. Thus, Confucian universalism allowed Nakamura to learn from the West while holding fast to the teachings of the East.

Late Tokugawa scholars like Nakamura could not only accommodate Western thought but were able to fuse it with Confucian universalism so as to forge a powerful philosophical foundation for Japan's rapid development into a modern world power. Sakatani Rōro's advocacy in 1874 of Japan's adoption of an Esperanto-like universal language in order to facilitate modernization and world unity is a vivid example of this dynamic at work.[18] At the age of fifty-one, this well known Confucian scholar, who had never studied a Western language, joined the Meirokusha, an intellectual society formed in 1874, which strongly advocated Western thought and institutions. Though Sakatani described himself as a "toothless old man" in the society's publication, his thought and that of his fellow member Nakamura Keiu represented the essential pedagogy of the society: it was necessary to create intelligent, moral men *and women* if Japan were to become a prosperous country.[19] The application of this principle was universal—it was true at any time for any person in any place. But the ethics that supported it was intensely individualistic. All men and women must help *themselves* to become energetic, industrious, and perseverant. As *Self Help* taught, "the wise and active conquer difficulties by daring to attempt them: sloth and folly shiver and shrink at the sight of toil and danger, and *make* the impossibility they fear."[20]

Though all men under heaven were capable of leading moral lives, all did not follow the laws of God, according to teachers like Nakamura and Smiles. In Nakamura's "Treatise on the Oneness of Morals and Happiness" a clear distinction was made between those who follow the laws of God and those who do not. This treatise teaches that if one were to walk the Path of Heaven, he would have abounding inner happiness *(nai fuku)*, while if he should stray, he would live in the depths of despair.[21] The treatise ends with a quotation from the Bible: "Every good tree bringeth forth good fruit; but a corrupt tree bringeth forth evil fruit."[22] Smiles warns, "Is there one whom difficulties dishearten—who bends to the storm? He will do little." But he adds, "Is there one who *will* conquer? That kind of man never fails."[23]

Individualistic ethics can easily be extremely elitist. And though the Ōyōmei monistic tendencies in Nakamura might appear to be more equalitarian than Smiles's Calvanism, the net result was the support of an intellectual and moral aristocracy. The Meirokusha constantly lamented the fact that they lived in a society where there were so few intelligent, moral men and so many who were unintelligent and morally degenerate. In his "Treatise on Changing the Character of the Japanese People," Nakamura bitterly denounced the immorality of most of his countrymen. He noted that since the Meiji Restoration in 1868, the form of government within which the people existed had greatly improved, but the Japanese character had remained unchanged. Then he unleashed his tirade: "They are still illiterate and culturally blind . . . ; they still indulge in wine and women . . . ; they still hate to read things . . . ; they don't know the way of heaven—they have no morals; they don't pay attention to their work; they are an unintelligent, narrow-minded people."[24]

Fukuzawa Yukichi, a Meirokusha colleague of Nakamura's who has been hailed as a crusader for the common people of Japan, consistently referred to those he championed as stupid people *(gu min)*. He stated, in his famous work *The Encouragement of Learning*, that it was because of their stupidity and lack of preseverance that the poor had become impoverished. Fukuzawa felt that they had no one to blame but themselves for their despicable state and even went so far as to warn that the only method to rule stupid people was by brute force.[25] Fukuzawa was by no means advocating a heavy-handed government for Japan—what he and Nakamura wanted was a nation of well-educated, moral people who would become capable of ruling themselves. However, early Meiji Confucian modernizers felt that the Japanese people had a long way to go before they could stand on their own feet. In the past, individual growth had been stunted by a feudal system that placed arbitrary class and hereditary distinctions above individual ability and virtue, but these restrictions, Nakamura and his Meirokusha colleagues thought, had been eliminated by the Meiji government. Liberty and equality were things that had to be won by each individual through his own merit. Unfortunately, few Japanese were able to meet the test.

Nishimura Shigeki, another Confucian scholar of the time, wrote numerous essays in the *Meiroku Magazine*, calling the Japanese people only half enlightened *(han kai ka)*. He ranked them well below the English. In fact, he even pleaded that because of the decadance of the Japanese, which he attributed to their sloth and illiteracy, it was necessary for Japan to impose high tariffs upon goods from nations where the populace was more intelligent and industrious or the effect upon Japanese economy would be disastrous.[26]

Samuel Smiles would have agreed with Nishimura's high opinion of the English. In *Self Help*, he stated: "The spirit of self-help, as exhibited in the energetic action of individuals, has in all times been a marked feature in the English character, and furnishes the true measure of our power as a nation."[27] England's corporate virtue, according to Smiles, was both established and maintained by a moral aristocracy who guided their countrymen by the example of their own superior conduct. Tokugawa-Meiji Confucianists had no difficulty understanding Smiles's quotation on "The True Gentlemen" *(Shinsei no kanshi)* when he read Nakamura's translation of *Self Help*:

> That which raises a country, that which strengthens a country, and that which dignifies a country—that which spreads her power, creates her moral influence, and makes her respected and submitted to, bends the heart of millions, and bows down the pride of nations to her—the instrument of obedience, the fountain of supremacy, the true throne, crown, and sceptre of a nation;—this aristocracy is not an aristocracy of blood, not an aristocracy of fashion, not an aristocracy of talent only; it is an aristocracy of Character. That is the true heraldry of man.[28]

Nakamura and Smiles agreed that strong nations could be built only by good works. Good works were done by men, not institutions. It was the responsibility of the intelligent and the virtuous to educate their countrymen, and if the people were properly receptive to their enlightened teaching, the whole nation would prosper. Just as an individual was known by his works, so was a nation. A virtuous nation, one whose people displayed the attributes of industry, patience, and perseverance, would bear good fruit. This was precisely what Nakamura meant when, in 1859, he counseled the Tokugawa leaders to dig a well in order to nourish their drought-ridden land. The Way of Heaven was the ultimate source of all virtue, wisdom, and power; and thus, reasoned Nakamura, the West's strength could only be due to one factor: its people were following the Way of Heaven. Smiles simply described the attributes of virtue and maintained that their energetic application would make men and nations prosperous. Nakamura, the Neo-Confucian scholar, indicated their source. In either case, the results were the same: virtue produced strength, and strength was a product of virtue. Furthermore, this dictum was as valid for nations as it was for individuals.

Neo-Confucian scholars such as Nakamura found their pre-Meiji education most useful in an era of rapid social and industrial development. More important, they helped lay the philosophical foundations for a powerful nation. William Elliot Griffis wondered if a nation could be born at once. His friend Nakamura Keiu helped make Japan into the kind of nation that Griffis greatly admired. As early as 1876, Griffis wrote of his wish that "the Sun-land lead the nations of Asia that are now appearing in the theatre of universal history," and he was a steadfast champion of Japan until his death fifty-two years later.[29] Nakamura Keiu did not live to see Japan's defeat of China in 1895, and it is doubtful if the victory of the Japanese nation-state over the land from which he received so much intellectual nourishment would have pleased him as it did his colleague Fukuzawa Yukichi. Fukuzawa hailed the victory as the result of perfect cooperation between the government and the people—a people and a government that were superior in wisdom and virtue to those of any nation in Asia.[30] But though Nakamura did not seem to share Fukuzawa's chauvinism, he still contributed significantly to Japan's emergence as a powerful nation-state. The evangelical ethic that he preached bore the same fruits in Japan as it did in the Anglo-Saxon nations. If strength was a product of virtue, then by the turn of the century Japan had indeed become the most virtuous nation in Asia.

NOTES

1. William Elliot Griffis, *The Mikado's Empire* (New York, 1877), p. 10.

2. *Ibid.*

3. One of the most fascinating tales of Meiji Japan is told by Takahashi in his autobiography, *Takahashi Korekiyo ji den* (Tokyo, 1936).

4. Fukuzawa Yukichi, *Gakumon no susume* (Tokyo, 1967 ed.), p. 102.

5. Nakamura Keiu, "Yōgaku ron," quoted in Ōkubo Toshiaki, "Nakamura Keiu no shoki yōgaku shisō to *Saikoku risshi hen* no yakujutsu oyobi kankō: Jakkan no shiryō no skōkai to sono kentō," *Shien*, 26.2–3:155 (Jan. 1966).

6. Samuel Smiles, *The Autobiography of Samuel Smiles, LL.D.* (New York, 1905), pp. 390–91.

7. Nakamura Keiu, "Jimmin no seishitsu o kaizō suru setsu," *Meiroku zasshi*, No. 30 (Feb. 1875), *Meiji bunka zenshū*, Vol. 5: *Zasshi hen* (Tokyo, 1955), p. 201.

8. For further information on the continuing success of *Saikoku risshi hen* and its importance during the Meiji era, see Shōwa Joshi Daigaku Kindai Bungaku Kenkyū Shitsu, *Nakamura Keiu, Kindai bungaku kenkyū sōsho*, 1:434–43 (Tokyo, 1956).

9. *Encylcopædia Britannica*, 11th ed. (1911), s.v. "Samuel Smiles." *Self Help* was most recently published in English in 1968.

10. Samuel Smiles, *Self Help: With Illustrations of Character, Conduct, and Perseverance* (New York, 1870), p. 21.

11. Nakamura, "Jimmin no seishitsu o kaizō suru setsu," p. 202.

12. Shōwa Joshi Daigaku Kindai Bungaku Kenkyū Shitsu, *Nakamura Keiu*, pp. 407–8.

13. Both Ishii Kendō and Takahashi Masao, who have written biographies of Nakamura, describe Nakamura as an exceptionally moral person. Hiyane Antei, the late authority on Japanese religion, once remarked that Nakamura was extremely "upright and uninteresting." For more on Nakamura's character, see Ishii Kendō, *Jijoteki jimbutsu tenkei Nakamura Masanao den* (Tokyo, 1907), and Takahasi Masao, *Nakamura Keiu* (Tokyo, 1966).

14. Though Satō Issai taught Ōyōmei, a heterodox school of Neo-Confucian thought, he also was well versed in orthodox Shu Shi (Chu Hsi) teachings, which were the official and supposedly the only doctrines taught at the Shōheikō. Many late Tokugawa Japanese Confucian scholars developed an appreciation for both schools. Nakamura was one of these scholars, as was Sakuma Shōzan, another of Sato Issai's famous students. For a discussion of Sato Issai's thought, see Inoue Tetsujirō, *Nihon Ōyōmei gakuha no tetsugaku* (Tokyo, 1938), pp. 225–59. Although Inoue includes a chapter on Nakamura in his *Nihon Shu Shi gakuha no tetsugaku* (Tokyo, 1905), he points out that Nakamura was not a strict follower of the orthodox school.

15. Nakamura's Christian ties are stressed and documented in Takahashi's *Nakamura Keiu.*

16. Nakamura Keiu, "Tokufu gōitsu no setsu," *Keiu Nakamura sensei enzetsushū*, quoted in Inoue Tetsujirō, *Nihon Shu Shi gakuha no tetsugaku*, pp. 569–82.

17. The philosophy of Wang Yang Ming is often referred to as the school of Universal Mind.

18. Sakatani Rōro, "Shitsugi issoku," *Meiroku zasshi*, No. 10, p. 107 (June 1874).

19. Sakatani's reference to himself is found in the last article of the *Meiroku zasshi*: "Sonnō jōi setsu," *Meiroku zasshi*, No. 43, p. 263 (Nov. 1875). Though Meirokusha members were strong advocates of women's education, their reasons for schooling women would be strongly criticized by most educators today. Women, they felt, must be educated so that Japan would be able to raise more enlightened men. One of the best statements of this position is Nakamura's "Treatise on How to Make Virtuous Mothers" (Zenryō naru haha o tsukuru setsu), *Meiroku zasshi*, No. 33, pp. 212–13 (Mar. 1875).

20. Smiles quotes this poem, which he attributes to Rowe. Smiles, *Self Help*, p. 346.

21. Nakamura, "Tokufu gōitsu no setsu," pp. 574–77.

22. *Ibid.*, p. 583. The English translation used is from the King James Bible, Matthew 7:17.

23. Smiles quotes a poem attributed to John Hunter, Smiles, *Self Help*, p. 346.

24. Nakamura, "Jimmin no seishitsu o kaizō suru setsu," p. 201.

25. Fukuzawa Yukichi, *Gakumon no susume*, pp. 17–18.

26. Nishimura Shigeki, "Jiyū kōeki ron," *Meiroku zasshi*, No. 29, pp. 194–96 (Feb. 1875).

27. Smiles, *Self Help*, p. 25.

28. Smiles, *ibid.*, p. 417, attributes this to *The Times*. Nakamura's translation is found in Samuel Smiles, *Saikoku risshi hen*, trans. Nakamura (Tokyo, 1876), p. 691.

29. Griffis, *The Mikado's Empire*, p. 578.

30. In his autobiography, Fukuzawa spoke of his satisfaction with the progress of Japan and its people, which, he felt, was best indicated by Japan's victory over China (Fukuzawa Yukichi, *The Autobiography of Fukuzawa Yukichi*, trans. Kiooka Eiichi [Tokyo, 1960], pp. 333–35). Fukuzawa's pride in the accomplishments of his countrymen as contrasted with the weak and degenerate state of the Chinese and Koreans is also clearly illustrated in a number of essays he wrote for the *Jiji shimpō* in 1895. These are found in volume 15 of the *Fukuzawa Yukichi zenshū* (Tokyo, 1959).

55136

The Gandhian Ethic of Work in India

Joseph W. Elder
University of Wisconsin

Central Bible College Library
Springfield, Missouri

The understanding of religious ferment in Asia would be lessened without an attempt to take a comparative look at some effects of the evangelical ethic. For purposes of definition, let us call an evangelical ethic a religiously endorsed doctrine urging active participation in the secular world. Typically, an evangelical ethic includes hard work and self-denial as integral parts of the religious life. Alternatives to an evangelical ethic might include a religious ethic urging withdrawal from active participation in the world (for example, monasticism), a religious ethic urging the correct observance of established rituals or ceremonies (for example, when a religion stresses ethnic identity), or a religious ethic advocating harmony between man and his environment (for example, within a group that sees tensions or conflicts as the greatest evil).

To what extent did evangelical ethics in Asia arise spontaneously from within Asia and to what extent were they brought in from the outside? In the case of Sam Jordan, a missionary to Persia, it is clear that he brought the ethic with him from outside Asia. With Nakamura Keiu, outside Christian contact was again an important stimulus. But with Mohandas Gandhi, the picture is somewhat more ambiguous. Although an Indian, he spent important developing years outside India, in Britain and South Africa. Although a staunch Hindu, he admitted to being deeply influenced by other religions. In Gandhi's case, these considerations make it more difficult to determine whether his version of the evangelical ethic came from within or without Asia.

In trying to analyze the origins of Gandhi's evangelical ethic, let us begin by looking at those forces that Gandhi himself said were important determinants. Gandhi maintained that he first recognized the central importance of this ethic in 1904.

By then he had already achieved some prominence in South Africa. As a lawyer, he had defended the local Indian colony from its white oppressors and had helped form the National Indian Congress. He had drafted an Indian petition and had sent it to the South African legislature. During the Boer War, he had aided the British by organizing the Indian Ambulance Corps. He had opened a law office in Johannesburg and had established a weekly journal, *Indian Opinion.* But he had not formally recognized the evangelical ethic. Then, in his thirty-fifth year, Gandhi took the train from Johannesburg to Durban. Henry S. L. Polak, an English friend, saw him off at the station, leaving Gandhi with a book to read during the journey. The book was *Unto This Last* by John Ruskin, a British critic of art and architecture, an Oxford professor of art, a writer, and a social philosopher. Gandhi described his subsequent experience as follows:

> The book was impossible to lay aside, once I had begun it. It gripped me. Johannesburg to Durban was a twenty-four hours' journey. The train reached there in the evening. I could not get any sleep that night. I determined to change my life in accordance with the ideals of the book.
>
> I believe that I discovered some of my deepest convictions reflected in this great book of Ruskin, and that is why it so captured me and made me transform my life.
>
> The teachings of *Unto This Last* I understood to be:
>
> 1. That the good of the individual is contained in the good of all.
>
> 2. That a lawyer's work has the same value as the barber's inasmuch as all have the same right of earning their livelihood for their work.
>
> 3. That a life of labour, *i.e.*, the life of the tiller of the soil and the handicraftsman is the life worth living.
>
> The first of these I knew. The second I had only dimly realized. The third had never occurred to me. *Unto This Last* made it as clear as daylight for me that the second and the third were contained in the first. I arose with the dawn, ready to reduce these principles to practice.[1]

This book was a catalyst that triggered a chain of events in Gandhi's life. Later he discovered that the Russian writers Leo N. Tolstoy and, before him, T. M. Bondaref had discovered the same "divine law, that man must earn his bread by labouring with his own hands." But throughout his life Gandhi continued to give John Ruskin credit for his original enlightenment.

Gandhi's esteem for Ruskin's *Unto This Last* is especially remarkable in view of the fact that two of the three teachings Gandhi discovered in Ruskin's book bore little relation to what Ruskin had written.

The first teaching that Gandhi identified, "that the good of the individual is contained in the good of all," could be derived from Ruskin's statement that

> riches are a power like that of electricity, acting only through inequalities or negations of itself. The force of the guinea you have in your pocket depends wholly on the default of a guinea in your neighbour's pocket. If he did not want it, it would be of no use to you . . . the art of making yourself rich . . . is therefore equally and necessarily the art of keeping your neighbour poor.[2]

Interestingly enough, Gandhi maintained he knew this teaching before reading Ruskin.

The second teaching, "that a lawyer's work has the same value as the barber's inasmuch as all have the same right of earning their livelihood for their work," might have been traced by Gandhi to Ruskin's statement that "a labourer serves his country with his spade, just as a man in the middle ranks of life serves it with sword, pen, or lancet."[3] If so, then Gandhi seriously misinterpreted Ruskin, for Ruskin made it clear he did not believe that the work of the labourer and the work of the middle ranks had "the same value," as Gandhi concluded. Ruskin stated:

> I never said that a colonel should have the same pay as a private, nor a bishop the same pay as a curate. Neither did I say that more work ought to be paid as less work (so that the curate of a parish of two thousand souls should have no more than the curate of a parish of five hundred). But I said that, so far as you employ it at all, bad work should be paid no less than good work because the moment people know they have to pay the

> bad and good alike, they will try to discern the one from the other, and not use the bad.[4]

Later Ruskin added:

> If there be any one point insisted on throughout my works more frequently than another, that one point is the impossibility of Equality. My continual aim has been to show the eternal superiority of some men to others . . . and to show also the advisability of appointing such persons or person to guide, to lead, or on occasion even to compel and subdue, their inferiors, according to their own better knowledge and wiser will.[5]

The third teaching that Gandhi discovered in Ruskin, "that the . . . life of the tiller of the soil and the handicraftsman is the life worth living," was an invention purely of Gandhi's—not of Ruskin's. Ruskin did state:

> We need examples of people who, leaving Heaven to decide whether they are to rise in the world, decide for themselves that they will be happy in it, and have resolved to seek—not greater wealth, but simpler pleasure; not higher fortune, but deeper felicity; making the first of possessions, self-possession; and honouring themselves in the harmless pride and calm pursuits of peace.[6]

But such people need not be tillers of the soil or handicraftsmen. Moreover, throughout *Unto This Last* Ruskin referred to the importance of physicians, soldiers, curates, and writers in contrast to those who performed more menial tasks. And Ruskin concluded:

> Labour is the contest of the life of man with an opposite;—the term "life" including his intellect, soul, and physical power, contending with question, difficulty, trial, or material force.
>
> Labour is of a higher or lower order, as it includes more or fewer of the elements of life: and labour of good quality, in any kind, includes always as much intellect and feeling as will fully and harmoniously regulate the physical force.[7]

Perhaps the puzzle of Gandhi "misreading" Ruskin is partially explained by Gandhi's own statement that "I discovered some of my deepest convictions reflected in this great book of

Ruskin." In the final analysis, Gandhi did not receive direction from Ruskin. Rather, Gandhi found support from Ruskin for some of his own deepest convictions. The three teachings Gandhi identified were conclusions he himself had nearly reached by other means. Ruskin's book merely served as a catalyst for finally announcing these conclusions. Gandhi's only mistake was in attributing them to Ruskin rather than to himself. Perhaps the young Indian still needed support from a Western intellectual before publicizing ideas he felt differed so radically from those of most Western intellectuals.

Characteristically, once Gandhi was convinced of the validity of a position, he changed his life accordingly. With the help of some friends, he bought a farm near Phoenix, in the Transvaal, moved the presses and offices of the weekly journal *Indian Opinion* to the farm, and assigned equal monthly allowances of three pounds each to the composer, the editor, and the errand boy. In time, a small colony of Gandhi's friends and supporters moved out to the farm. Those with servants retained them, and those who were married continued to live in family units. On Phoenix farm Gandhi began some of his early experiments with grinding flour by hand. And Gandhi reports that here, in 1906, after he had adopted the vows of celibacy, he looked upon the Phoenix settlement as a religious institution.[8]

In 1910 Gandhi needed a base of operations closer to Johannesburg and to his campaign for equal treatment of Indians. Again, with the help of friends, Gandhi established Tolstoy farm twenty-one miles from Johannesburg, where he began more radical communal and economic experiments. Among the settlers were Hindus, Muslims, Christians, and Parsees. They prepared their own bread, marmalade, and caramel coffee, and made their own sandals and furniture. In organization, the farm was more self-consciously similar to the traditional Hindu ashrams of gurus and their disciples. Gandhi retained in his own hands the managing authority. There was to be no smoking or drinking. Vegetarianism was practiced even by Muslim members of the farm. For a time, no one even ate cooked foods or drank milk. One could use public transport only when on an errand for the commune; otherwise one had to walk. There were no servants; all work on the farm was done by the participants, including the disposal of waste and nightsoil.

The pattern of a religious cooperative community continued in Gandhi's later ashrams in India—Satyagraha ashram (first near Ahmedabad and later by the Sabarmati River), Wardha ashram, and finally Sevagram ashram in Segaon, a village close to Wardha, in central India. In these later ashrams Gandhi established regulations for all members, including vows of truth, nonviolence, celibacy, control of the palate, and *swadeshi* (using only local products).[9] He resorted to moral instruction and occasional personal fasting to encourage the observance of these vows. One of the goals of his later ashrams was to become an economically self-sufficient community that could serve as a blueprint for all of India's villages.

Within the context of experiences with his ashrams, Gandhi formulated the defining characteristics of what he called "bread labor." Bread labor, as Gandhi saw it, is a "divine law"—the principle that "to live man must work."[10] All work is not automatically bread labor, however. First, the work must involve bodily labor. When asked "May not men earn their bread by intellectual labor?" Gandhi replied: "Intellectual work is important and has an undoubted place in the scheme of life. But what I insist on is the necessity of physical labour. I venture to say that in ancient times, brahmanas worked with their body as with their mind. But even if they did not, body labour was a proved necessity at the time."[11] "The needs of the body must be supplied by the body."[12] To underscore his point, Gandhi insisted that even Nobel prizewinners like the poet Rabindranath Tagore and the mathematician C. V. Raman should earn their bread by manual labour.[13] Gandhi felt that at times he himself was deficient in this regard, spending his days meeting visitors, writing articles, and organizing movements rather than tilling the fields. In 1925 he said: "For me at the present moment spinning is the only body labour I give. It is a mere symbol. I do not give enough body labour."[14] For many Gandhians, spinning became a symbol they could observe in their homes before departing for a day of nonmanual work—again, a symbol of bread labour.

Second, work, to be bread labour, has to be voluntary. Gandhi wrote: "Compulsory obedience to a master is a state of slavery, willing obedience to one's father is the glory of sonship. Similarly, compulsory obedience to the law of bread labour breeds poverty, disease and discontent. It is a state of slavery. Willing obedience to it must bring contentment and health."[15] According to this, the millions of Indian peasants engaged in farming are not necessarily performing bread labour. They are working only out of necessity.

Third, bread labour has the goal of social service. Gandhi wrote:

> The ashram holds that every man and woman must work in order to live . . . every healthy individual must labour enough for his food, and his intellectual faculties must be exercised not in order to obtain a living or amass a fortune, but only in the service of mankind. If this principle is observed everywhere, all men would be equal, none would starve and the world would be saved from many a sin.[16]

Even the humblest peasant can turn his daily activities into bread labour if he recognizes that he is serving mankind through his work and then voluntarily continues to perform it. Gandhi's incorporation of social service into bread labour provided him with a moral base from which to reevaluate traditional Hinduism. Using his criteria of bread labour, Gandhi denounced the mendicants and the mendicant charity that centuries earlier had become an integral part of Hinduism:

> My friendship for the paupers of India has made me hard-hearted enough to contemplate their utter starvation with equanimity in preference to their utter reduction to beggary. My ahimsa ["nonviolence"] would not tolerate the idea of giving a free meal to a healthy person who has not worked for it in some honest way, and if I had the power, I would stop every sadavrata where free meals are given. It has degraded the nation and has encouraged laziness, idleness, hypocrisy and even crime. Such misplaced charity adds nothing to the wealth of the country, whether material or spiritual, and gives a false sense of meritoriousness to the donor . . . the rule should be, "No labour, no meal."[17]

Along the same lines, Gandhi denounced the life of withdrawal and contemplation that had been a part of classical religious life for nearly three thousand years: "If I had the good fortune to be face to face with one like [Buddha], I should not hesitate to ask him why he did not teach the gospel of work, in preference to one of contemplation. I should do the same thing if I were to meet [the great saints Tukaram and Dnyanadev]."[18]

Turning to his own gospel of work, Gandhi wrote: "If I could persuade myself that I should find Him [God] in a Himalayan cave I would proceed there immediately. But I know that I cannot find Him apart from humanity . . . the only way to find God is to see Him in His creation and be one with it. This can only be done by service of all."[19]

To an outside observer, Gandhi's focus on service-directed work was sharply different from the focus of most Hindu traditions. Early Hinduism had stressed sacrifice *(yajna)* and the tending of sacrificial fires. To this the *Upanishads* had added the importance of asceticism, withdrawal from the world, and salvation *(moksha)* through insight or knowledge. Later the *Bhagavad-Gita* had stressed man's correct performance of his birth-given tasks: the Brahmana to pray; the warrior to wage war; and so forth. "Better one's own duty, (tho) imperfect, than another's duty well performed; Better death in (doing) one's own duty; Another's duty brings danger" (III.35).[20] In the latter portions of the *Gita* a new path to salvation had been described, the path of *bhakti*, or devotion. During the next centuries, this path had become increasingly important, with man's most important religious activity being the passionate worship of God. Religious virtuosi now engaged in the establishment of devotional communities, where attention was focused on adoration and the search for a personal revelation of God. One might conclude that Gandhi's work ethic was compatible with none of these.

To draw such a conclusion, however, would be to overlook Gandhi's capacity to discover new meanings in old scriptures. Nowhere did he change his personal religious goal from the *moksha* goal of classical Hinduism: "What I want to achieve,—what I have been striving and pining to achieve these thirty years,—is self-realization, to see God face to face, to attain Moksha."[21]

However, his reinterpretations of certain scriptural passages so altered their original meanings that he was able to read them to support his doctrine of bread labour. For example, Gandhi reworked the meaning of sacrifice *(yajna)* as follows:

> [I] venture to suggest that in the verses 12 and 13 of chapter III (in the Gita) the word *yajna* is capable

> of only one meaning. The fourteenth verse makes it absolutely clear which means:
>
> "By food the living live; food comes of rain, and rain comes by the pious sacrifice, and sacrifice is paid with tithes of toil."—Arnold
>
> Here, therefore, there is not only the theory, in my opinion, of bodily labour propounded, but there is also the theory established of labour not only for oneself but for others, when and only when it becomes *yajna* or sacrifice.[22]

Similarly, Gandhi found roots for his doctrine of bread labour in the first verse of the *Ishopanishad*—a verse he felt summed up the whole of Hinduism. As Gandhi translated it, this *mantra* (verse) described the basic unity of Brahma and Atma: "All that there is in this universe, great or small, including the tiniest atom, is pervaded by God."[23] Gandhi went on from there to conclude: "This *mantra* tells me that I cannot hold as mine anything that belongs to God, and if my life and that of all who believe in this *mantra* has to be a life of perfect dedication, it follows that it will have to be a life of continual service to our fellow creatures."[24]

Gandhi was even able to reinterpret *bhakta* (devotee) and *bhakti* (devotion) in a way that supported his doctrine of bread labour.

> The Gita has defined the *bhakta* in three places. . . . But a knowledge of the definition of a *bhakta* is hardly a sufficient guide. They are rare on this earth. I have therefore suggested the Religion of Service as the Means. God of Himself seeks for His seat the heart of him who serves his fellowmen. That is why Narasinha Mehta who "saw and knew" sang "He is a true *Vaishnava* who knows to melt at other's woe." Such was Abu ben Adhem. He served his fellowmen, and therefore his name topped the list of those who served God. . . . He who spins before the poor inviting them to do likewise serves God as no one else does. "He who gives me even a trifle such as a fruit or a flower or even a leaf in the spirit of *bhakti* is My servant," says the Lord in the Bhagavadgita. And He hath His footstool where live "the humble, the lowliest and the lost." Spinning, therefore, for such is the greatest prayer, the greatest worship, the greatest sacrifice.[25]

In short, once having discovered his ethic of work or the doctrine of bread labour in the writings of Ruskin, Tolstoy, and Bondaref, Gandhi looked back into the classical Hindu scriptures and identified passages that also lent Hindu support to the doctrine. In Gandhi's eyes, *yajna* (sacrifice) became bread labour; recognition of the Brahma-Atma mystery led to bread labour; *bhakti* (devotion) *was* bread labour.

To return to a question raised early in this paper, to what extent did evangelical ethics arise spontaneously from within Asia and to what extent were they brought in from the outside? In Gandhi's case, the evangelical ethic he advocated emerged from a complex mixture of Asian and non-Asian sources. In his own words, he discovered some of his deepest convictions reflected in the writings of the non-Asians Ruskin, Tolstoy, and Bondaref. Closer examination indicates that the non-Asians may have provided legitimacy for his views, but his views had developed independently from the non-Asian authors he cited. They arose out of Gandhi's personal response to his childhood in India, youth in Britain, and early career in South Africa. Had Gandhi not read Ruskin, Tolstoy, and Bondaref, one might guess that he still would have eventually announced his views.

Once he had publicly declared his convictions, indicating their non-Asian roots, Gandhi then looked for parallel roots within the Hindu heritage. His search was successful. In such basic scriptures as the *Ishopanishad* and the *Bhagavad-Gita* he discovered statements supporting his doctrine of bread labour. These scriptures, in turn, provided him with the assumptions and figures of speech he used to preach this ethic to his countrymen. The following passage illustrates as eloquently as any the harmonious blend that Gandhi created:

> It has been truly said, that desire for enjoyment creates bodies for the soul. When this desire vanishes, there remains no further need for the body, and man is free from the vicious cycle of births and deaths. . . . We thus arrive at the ideal of total renunciation, and learn to use the body for the purposes of service so long as it exists. . . . Every moment of our life should be filled with mental or physical activity. . . . One who has consecrated his life to service cannot be idle for a single moment.[26]

NOTES

1. M. K. Gandhi, *An Autobiography: The Story of My Experiments with Truth*, 2d ed. (Ahmedabad, 1940), pp. 298–99.

2. John Ruskin, *Unto This Last: Four Essays on the First Principles of Political Economy* (New York, 1872), pp. 44, 45.

3. *Ibid.*, p. xiii.

4. *Ibid.*, p. 82*n*.

5. *Ibid.*, p. 87.

6. *Ibid.*, p. 135.

7. *Ibid.*, p. 113.

8. M. K. Gandhi, *Ashram Observances in Action*, trans. Valji G. Desai (Ahmedabad, 1955), p. 4.

9. *Ibid.*, pp. 125–51.

10. M. K. Gandhi, *From Yeravda Mandir*, trans. Valji G. Desai, 3d ed. (Ahmedabad, 1945), p. 35.

11. *Harijan*, Feb. 23, 1947, p. 36, cited in M. K. Gandhi *Bread Labour (The Gospel of Work)* (Ahmedabad, 1960), p. 18.

12. *Harijan*, June 29, 1935, cited in Gandhi, *Bread Labour*, p. 17.

13. *Harijan*, Feb. 23, 1947, cited in Gandhi, *Bread Labour*, p. 18.

14. *Young India*, Nov. 5, 1925, cited in Gandhi, *Bread Labour*, p. 16.

15. *Harijan*, June 29, 1935, p. 156, cited in M. K. Gandhi, *Economic and Industrial Life and Relations* (Ahmedabad, 1957), I, 98–99.

16. Gandhi, *Ashram Observances in Action*, p. 60.

17. *Young India*, Aug. 13, 1925, cited in Gandhi, *Economic and Industrial Life and Relations*, I, 128–29.

18. *Harijan*, Nov. 2, 1935, p. 298, cited in Gandhi, *Economic and Industrial Life and Relations*, I, 127.

19. *Harijan*, Aug. 29, 1936, p. 226, cited in Nirmal Kumar Bose, ed., *Selections from Gandhi*, 2d ed. (Ahmedabad, 1957), p. 25.

20. Franklin Edgerton, trans., *The Bhagavad-Gita*, Vol. 38 of the Harvard Oriental Series, ed. Walter E. Clark (Cambridge, Mass., 1952), III.35, p. 39.

21. Gandhi, *An Autobiography*, p. xii.

22. *Young India*, Oct. 15, 1925, p. 355, cited in Gandhi, *Bread Labour*, p. 10.

23. *Harijan*, Jan. 30, 1937, p. 407, cited in Gandhi, *Bread Labour*, p. 6.

24. *Harijan*, Jan. 30, 1937, cited in M. K. Gandhi, *The Gospel of Renunciation* (Ahmedabad, 1961), p. 11.

25. *Young India*, Sept. 24, 1925, pp. 331–32, cited in M. K. Gandhi, *My God* (Ahmedabad, 1962), p. 43.

26. Gandhi, *From Yeravda Mandir*, pp. 25–26.

The Religious Meaning of Ch'oe Che-u's Tonghak Doctrine, 1860-1864

Key Ray Chong
Texas Tech University

Until the middle of the nineteenth century Korea had experienced and had experimented with various alien doctrines: religious, political, social, or otherwise. Three major Chinese doctrines—Confucianism, Taoism, and Buddhism—were introduced into Korea during the period of the Three Kingdoms in Korea, which lasted until the unification of Korea by the Silla in A.D. 668. The Silla dynasty (57 B.C. to A.D. 931), which was one of the Three Kingdoms, became a patron of Chinese teachings, particularly Buddhism. As a result, the succeeding dynasty, Koryo (918 to 1392), continued to promote Buddhism at the expense of the other two. After the Yi dynasty (1392 to 1910) came to power in the fourteenth century, the more politically oriented Neo-Confucianism (Chu Hsi's version) began to enjoy the patronage of the ruling elite and the scholars of the time. During the following five-hundred-year reign of the Yi house the religiously oriented doctrines of Buddhism, Taoism, and shamanism of a Korean version were pushed into the background, if not completely eliminated, by the ruling elite *(yangban)*. But in the teeth of official persecution, they managed to survive, and in the middle of the nineteenth century they found a patron in the person of Ch'oe Che-u. Not only did he synthesize all three Chinese teachings plus Korean and Western religions, but he also provided the people with spiritual inspiration and guidance.

Ch'oe Che-u's Tonghak doctrine, known as "Eastern Learning," was created in 1860. Since then it has undergone a series of changes in its theory and practice. Historically, at least in the very beginning, it began as a religious teaching composed of the major and minor existing cultures (Confucianism, Buddhism, Taoism, shamanism, and traditionalism) together with Christianity, which was introduced into Korea in the nineteenth century. The initial Tonghak doctrine was not only eclectic but also religious. It encouraged its followers to rely on personal salvation and/or self-enlightenment rather than on external authority for their answers to the problems of life. It did not defy or reject the existing political regime, nor did it believe that political reform could result in peace of mind for the individual.

Recent scholarship has stressed the political and social elements of the Tonghak doctrine. This emphasis is understandable, because the later Tonghak movement became a popular political movement and finally culminated in the form of a prototype of the Korean nationalist movement in the wake of the Sino-Japanese War of 1895.[1] The later Tonghak movement, indeed, was religious as well as political and social in nature, but the earlier movement and doctrine were more religious and ethical than otherwise. The confusion arose from the fact that the later followers of the Tonghak doctrine became more politically and socially concerned. And then they incorporated their own ideas into the Tonghak doctrine. Ch'oe Si-hyong, Chon Pong-chun, and Son Pyong-hi are good examples of the above development. They all contributed to the later version of the Tonghak doctrine during the late nineteenth and early twentieth centuries.

Therefore, the purpose of this study is not to treat the early Tonghak doctrine as a political and social gospel but rather as a religious and ethical teaching. To do this, I will proceed with the assumption that there are internal standards of validity in ideas themselves[2] and also that ideas are functions of the persons who express them and the shape that ideas take is relative to the culture and era in which they develop and are used.[3] I will reject the assumption that ideas or doctrines can be understood only within the context of the prevailing political, social, economic, and cultural realities. Often there is a danger that this will lead to a discussion in terms of causes and effects, that is, that realities are the causes while ideas are the effects. A study of ideas themselves may provide us with valuable clues, though not complete answers, to the problems resulting from and/or related to the ideas.

In studying the Tonghak doctrine of Ch'oe Che-u, one is struck immediately by the fact that its sources are numerous. Confucianism, Taoism, Buddhism, and Christianity were assimilated into what was known as indigenous Korean shamanism and traditionalism. As a result, all these teachings, except

Christianity, became an integral and inseparable part of Korean culture. In view of this fact, it is extremely difficult for us to separate one source from the other, and it is equally difficult to define or trace back the meaning of the concepts as found in the Tonghak doctrine. An idea borrowed from one source was frequently blended with a concept adapted from another. Thus, not only was the resulting syncretism or synthesis taken for granted, but it was also impossible to relate the ideas to their original sources. For example, the Korean term for heaven *(ch'on)* originated either in Chinese classics or in indigenous Korean myths, but it could also refer to a Christian heaven. In other words, Tonghak terms or concepts may have contained many different connotations and denotations taken from Chinese, Korean, and Christian sources. The Tonghak conception of heaven cannot be entirely Eastern or Western but is a synthesis of both. To take another example, the term Confucianism *(yuhak* or *yukyo)* may mean the philosophy of any Confucianist (Confucius, Mencius, Hsün Tzu, Tung Chung-shu, Chu Hsi, or Wang Yang-ming), or it may mean a combination of the ideas of two or three of these Confucianists. Diversity of content is also seen in Buddhism, Taoism, shamanism, and traditionalism, from which Tonghak derives its main ideas.

These difficulties in understanding the Tonghak doctrine are intensified as a result of Ch'oe Che-u's explanations of certain Tonghak ideas and quotations from Chinese, Korean, and Christian sources. His expositions and quotations are unsystematic and unclear. This makes it difficult for us to establish conceptual connections between an idea and its source, or the exact origin of the idea within a given conceptual framework. To be more specific, Ch'oe Che-u, the initial interpreter of the Tonghak doctrine, seldom gave credit to other thinkers or to what they had done. Instead, he treated the borrowed ideas as if they were his own. Last but not least, our study of the Tonghak doctrine is further complicated by our own misunderstanding, if not distortion, which is the result of differences in time and place.

The initial Tonghak doctrine expounded by Ch'oe Che-u was apolitical. Ch'oe is said to have received "divine revelations" in 1860. Until then he had wandered around many parts of Korea in search of spiritual enlightenment, visiting many famous Buddhist temples, mountains, rivers, and people. After 1860 he began to explain the religious experiences and spiritual enlightenment in terms of what he called Tonghak (Eastern Learning). Yet his supporters soon became political outcasts to the government because of their support of Roman Catholicism, which had been banned for some time. Ironically, the Tonghaks were regarded as pro-Christian and responsible for disgracing Neo-Confucianism, which had been officially considered orthodox. They did not challenge the government authority or defy the status quo, and yet their leader, Ch'oe Che-u, was arrested and summarily executed in 1864.[4]

The government accused Ch'oe and his followers of using such terms as Heavenly Master *(ch'onchu)* and Supreme Lord *(sangche)* in reference to God or heaven, expressions widely used by Korean Catholics. Being afraid of possible government persecutions, Ch'oe consciously played down the importance of Christianity, an increasingly popular religion in Korea. He called his teaching Tonghak, or Eastern Learning, as opposed to Sohak, or Western Learning. The purpose of such gestures was obviously to mollify the government and at the same time to impress its anti-Christian officials. Having witnessed the Christian-inspired Taiping Rebellion in China and having been disturbed by the event, Ch'oe became increasingly and openly hostile to Christianity on the grounds that it was too politically motivated. Ch'oe said:

> Late in 1860 I heard rumor that Occidental people take no interest in wealth and high positions in order to fulfill the will of Heavenly Master. Yet they conquered the world [referring to China] to establish churches and propagate their Way [meaning Christianity]. Thus I began to question why the Western Way had been so [aggressive and mean].[5]

It appears that Ch'oe detested the politically, economically, and religiously aggressive nature of Christianity and of the Western powers connected with it. At the same time, he tried to underscore the importance of his Tonghak doctrine in coping with the situation in Korea, but only in a spiritual or religious way. He hinted that "his object was the maintenance of all the old national customs and religion, as against Christianity and its doctrine, which was then gaining some ground."[6]

But on the other hand Ch'oe did not, and perhaps could not, eliminate Christian elements from his thinking. Despite his personal antipathy toward Christianity, there is considerable evidence of Christian elements in Ch'oe's Tonghak doctrine. For example, the story of Ch'oe's conversion or revelation in 1860 so closely resembles the account given by St. Paul that it seems likely that Ch'oe borrowed the story without acknowledging the source. A comparison of the two versions of conversion is illuminating:

> Suddenly there shined round about him a light from heaven . . . and [Paul] heard a voice saying unto him, Saul, Saul, why persecutest thou me? And he said, Who art thou Lord? And the Lord said, I am Jesus whom thou persecutest. . . . And he trembling and astonished said, Lord, what wilt thou have me to do? And the Lord said unto him, Arise, and go into the city, and it shall be told thee what thou must do. Acts 9:3–6.

> Suddenly in April my heart shuddered and my body trembled . . . in the midst of this experience my ears suddenly heard a mysterious voice which said: "Do not be frightened. The people in this world called me the Supreme Lord. Then why did you not know who I am?" I asked the Supreme Lord why He chose to speak to me in this way and He answered: "I myself could have accomplished little, and so decided to send you to the world to teach my Law to all." [Pp. 16–17]

While acknowledging some similarities between his doctrine and Christianity, Ch'oe felt that the differences were more important: "Their [Christians'] purpose is similar to mine, but they do not have truth [in their doctrine]" (pp. 27–28). Moreover, Christians had no logical sequence in their speech and their written works, nor did they have proper decorum in their worship of God. Even worse, they used prayer for selfish ends, and their knowledge of God was superficial and distorted. When Ch'oe was asked if his teachings were Western, he emphatically retorted: "My answer is no, because I was born in the East and received the Way in the East. Thus my Way is the Heavenly Way and my Learning is the Eastern Learning." He continued: "As you see, the land is divided into East and West. Then how can we say that West is East and East is West. . . . I received my Way in this land, and will propagate my Way in this land. Then how can I call my Way Western?" (p. 29).

Despite his emphasis on the differences, when asked why people in the world did not respect the Heavenly Lord *(ch'on-chu)*, Ch'oe replied, "It is human nature that the first time most people ask for the Heavenly Lord is at their deathbed" (p. 32). He then alluded to the biblical story in which one of the two thieves who was being crucified with Jesus pleaded with Him, "Lord, remember me when thou comest into thy kingdom" (Luke 23:42). Like Jesus, Ch'oe made clear that his mission was to save his followers by spiritual enlightenment rather than political reform, for he doubted the efficiency or effectiveness of politics in improving the conditions of his followers. What Ch'oe really desired was the creation of a peaceful spiritual state of mind rather than a materially prosperous but secular state on earth.

The same reasoning can be found in Ch'oe's discussions on Confucianism. According to Ch'oe, the cardinal principles of Tonghak are found in the traditional Confucian relationships of king to subject, father to son, husband to wife, aged to young, and friend to friend. A realization of these relationships can only come from self-cultivation *(susin)*, thereby enabling man and heaven to become one and the same (p. 85). This idea of self-cultivation also indicates Ch'oe's willingness to make a gradual change in the minds and spirits of individuals rather than a drastic change in society and government (p. 31). In the spring of 1860 Ch'oe received a revelation from heaven and also learned, after an extensive study of the *Book of Changes* (*Ikyong*; *I-ching* in Chinese), that if a person controlled and constantly improved himself, then nothing would prevent realization of his aspirations. Here again, Ch'oe seems reluctant to admit that the idea of self-cultivation came from Confucian classics. What Ch'oe simply said was that if a person studied Confucian teachings carefully, he would find them not only reasonable but also very similar to Ch'oe's Tonghak doctrine (pp. 42–43).

From the above it is also clear that Ch'oe did not advocate a radical change in the government and society in either theory or practice, but that he approved of Confucianism as a means of spiritual self-improvement, although the latter had become the basis of the socio-economic-political systems of the time. It is difficult to identify completely Ch'oe's views with the initial version of Confucianism, and consequently his version of Confucianism became increasingly difficult to label. In his description of the role of man, for example, Ch'oe asserted that the two principles, both positive and negative *(umyang)*, had produced hundreds of thousands of things, of which man was the most spiritual and perfect being; for man had established and had clarified the laws and functions of heaven, earth, and man, along with the five agents *(ohaeng)* (p. 22). When asked why the mind of heaven was the mind of man and why there were both good and bad, Ch'oe replied that the virtue of a princely man *(kuncha)* was in union with the virtue of heaven and earth, while the virtue of a mean man was in discord with the virtue of heaven and earth. Only the will of the Heavenly Master alone could dictate the course of all these events (p. 31). In general, Ch'oe sounds like the Han Confucianist Tung Chung-shu, who had discussed the role of man and his relationship to heaven and earth and the five agents.

Ch'oe also stressed the perfection of self through the cultivation of belief *(sin)* and sincerity *(song)*, both of which required serious self-discipline and study. He argued that man should be armed with the strong senses of belief and sincerity in order to distinguish between good and evil. He believed that man could develop belief and sincerity simultaneously, because these were closely related not only etymologically but also in the process of learning and practicing. The character belief means the words of man, whereas sincerity means the fulfillment of his words. By this, Ch'oe meant the people should value the importance of self-perfection through the process of education. On another occasion he repeated the same theme: every individual should make his maximum effort for self-perfection, since emperors and scholars created laws and institutions for the benefit of the people (p. 51). In his *Song of Admonition (Kyohunka)* Ch'oe stressed the five Confucian ethics *(oryun)* as a means to achieve self-perfection (p. 84). But he did not fail to point out how difficult it was to follow these Confucian teachings, remarking that "only seventy-two out of three thousand candidates had really become good students of Confucius" (pp. 99–101). The reason for such selectivity was that "heaven only helps those who have accomplished self-cultivation from time immemorial" (pp. 99–101). For this reason Ch'oe believed that only those who had achieved self-cultivation through their own efforts could enjoy happiness as such.

In discussing the attainment of the Way *(to)*, derived from the Confucian classic the *Great Mean* (*Chungyong*; *Chung-yung* in Chinese), Ch'oe suggested that one should simply identify himself with the Way of Heaven with all his heart, spirit, honor, benevolence, righteousness, propriety, and wisdom plus sincerity and respect (p. 118). He added that, however, it would be hard to do so, because man often would find it difficult to act upon anything in this world (p. 120).

From the preceding remarks, one can see similarities in the attainment of the Way between Ch'oe and Wang Yang-ming in style and logic when it comes to self-cultivation or self-perfection. For example, Wang believed that self-cultivation leading to the attainment of the Way would serve the purpose of improving both state and society. But on the other hand, Ch'oe felt that this kind of spiritual change in the hearts and minds of the people would be conducive to and tolerable to the existing regime, because he regarded it as within the framework of the old order. Noticeable is the fact that the manner in which Confucianism was treated by Ch'oe was far more religious and ethical than political, while Wang was more politically and ethically oriented than otherwise in his treatment of Confucianism.

Then how did Ch'oe use or incoporate Buddhist concepts into the making of his Tonghak doctrine? Here again, Ch'oe used and synthesized Buddhist elements into his own religious and ethical doctrine. Although Buddhist ideas as such are minimal in the Tonghak doctrine, such Tonghak concepts as heart-cleansing and bodily purification seem to be related to and derived from Buddhism. The following example is typical: Ch'oe urged his followers to "rectify the crooked minds so as to grasp truth. . . . Ridding [ourselves of] dirty minds, let us cultivate gentle and good minds with all our hearts" (p. 58). He also urged them to believe in the Way, not to study it. But Ch'oe did not acknowledge his indebtedness to Buddhism, nor did he refer to it. What is surprising is that Buddhist concepts such as merit-making (*kongtak*; *kung-te* in Chinese—the translation of *karma* in Sanskrit) are distorted from their original meanings. While the Buddhists used and advocated merit-making as opposed to simple faith in the process of attaining spiritual salvation (*nirvana* in Sanskrit), Ch'oe simply regarded it as one of many means "to facilitate the attainment of one's perfect mind" (p. 110). Also, Buddhist elements took the form of a synthesis blended with a kind of Confucianism. Ch'oe stated: "Benevolence, righteousness, propriety and wisdom . . . were taught by wise men of ancient times [referring to Confucius and his disciples] but self-cultivation *(susin)* and rightful mind *(chongki)* were solely created by myself" (p. 45).

All these concepts were a mixture of both Confucian and Buddhist ideas, yet Ch'oe did not identify the sources of these concepts. Besides, Ch'oe, to our amazement, treated the law of purifying one's body from natural and moral filth as a Taoist idea.[7] All these statements suggest that there were at least two things in Ch'oe's mind. One is that the concept of purification had three elements: that is, Confucianism, Taoism, and Buddhism, which were blended together. The other is that Ch'oe himself was uncertain of the exact origins of these ideas. Thus, perhaps Ch'oe did not know the original or intended meaning of these terms.

In the opening pages of the "Essay on the Propagation of Virtues" *(potokmun)*, Ch'oe, perhaps unintentionally, admitted that his doctrine had been strongly colored by Taoist views, particularly his doctrine on life and nature. He wrote of nature: "From time immemorial spring and autumn have come and gone. The four seasons are evidence of the Heavenly Master's art of creation demonstrated to the world." "People," he continued, "left the course of each action and inaction and each victory and defeat as well, to the mercy of Heavenly Mandate *(ch'onmyong)*. . . . A man would become a princely man if he would have fulfilled the principles of Way and Virtue" (pp. 13–14). Ch'oe's views of nature were a potpourri of Taoist and Confucian elements, for his views in many respects parallel those of Taoists, particularly those of Lao Tzu. But there were some differences in his understanding of nature and man. For example, Ch'oe believed that the laws that affected changes in nature were immutable, but he did believe that those governing man's moral character could be altered. To put it differently, the former can be compared to those of Taoism, whereas the latter can be compared to those of Confucianism. But at times he did not separate one from the other in his use of the laws. For example, he described a princely man *(kuncha)* as a man who submitted himself to the Heavenly Principle *(ch'onli)* or the Heavenly Mandate *(ch'onmyong)* (p. 15). Obviously Ch'oe is referring to Confucian natural laws, because Taoism itself does not emphasize human submission to and reverence for a physical entity of any kind. This assumption can be made from the fact that Ch'oe implied that the Way and Virtue were a kind of human effort to fulfill certain tangible requirements necessary for communion with the Tao, or "Superior One," who would and could perfect humanity. However, Ch'oe did not view Way and Virtue as the metaphysical Taoist concepts of the *Tao* and *Te*, which exist above and beyond human conception and control.[8]

In his "Essay on Learning" *(nonhakmun)* Ch'oe again demonstrated his synthesis of both Confucianism and Taoism when he described the role of man in the universe and the nature of the universe:

> Man (sage) established and clarified the laws of the three geniuses: heaven, earth and man. He also created the principles of the five agents. What are the five agents? Heaven is the source that operates the five agents; earth is the foundation that makes them; man is the representative of them. With these five agents the laws of the three geniuses—heaven, earth and man—can be perceived. Four seasons have come and gone; wind, dew, frost and snow have never understood such secrets of nature. Some people said these were nothing but spontaneous creations of the law of nature. Whether these were the blessings of the Heavenly Master or not, we cannot see them. Even if these were spontaneous creations of the Heavenly Master, it is too mysterious to describe them in words. The reason is that from ancient times until now nobody has yet unlocked the secret laws of nature. [Pp. 22–23]

Ch'oe understood the creation of the universe more or less in Taoist terms. In his comments on the tangible results that nature produced, Ch'oe referred to heaven and earth, and yet he did not distinguish between the intangible Creator of heaven and earth and the eternal or unnamable Way from which all emanated (pp. 50, 52, 54). Therefore the above quotation conveys the impression that the kind of Confucianism Ch'oe had in mind was Tung Chung-shu's version of "Han" Confucianism, because of his lengthy remarks on Taoism and his frequent use of the five agents.[9]

The story that Ch'oe was immortal or a fairy *(sonin)* also gives us certain parallels between Ch'oe and Chuang Tzu. Like the Taoists, Ch'oe compared himself to an immortal being and also to a dragon or tiger: "I am an immortal being . . . and I can be either a tiger or a dragon [at the same time]" (pp. 73,

79, 118). He went on to say that as an immortal being he possessed the powers of a sorcerer as well as the vision of a messiah and could even provide elixirs and panaceas (pp. 79, 80, 89).

Upon reading this passage we are immediately reminded of the popular Taoist stories in which Chuang Tzu, a student of Lao Tzu, turned into a butterfly and in which the later Taoists promised to provide either elixirs or panaceas. But there are vast differences between the two. As for Ch'oe, he went one step farther than the Taoists. First, he asserted that man transformed himself into an immortal being, or a dragon or a tiger, in order that heaven and man could communicate with each other in spirit and body. Second, based on this assertion, Ch'oe advanced a more audacious idea; that is, the idea of *innaech'on*, which means that both heaven and man are one and the same (pp. 25, 31–32).

From the above it appears that Ch'oe did not regard Buddhism or Taoism as political or social doctrines. Ch'oe did not suggest any political or economic reforms for improving peoples' lives. Instead, men should look inwardly and transcend the realities of life in searching for solutions to all of their problems. Throughout his discussions on Buddhism and Taoism, Ch'oe very seldom made any attempts to relate them to an improvement of the state and society.

Ch'oe, himself the proud possessor of elixirs and a sojourner to the world of the spirit, was also interested in the so-called shamanism inherent in the traditional customs and practices of Korea. Shamanism, by definition, is a primitive religion of northeast Asia in which those who call themselves shamans act as both priests and medicine men, possessing spiritual and healing powers respectively. They also communicate with supernatural forces, both good and evil. Here again, Ch'oe incorporated some of the indigenous shamanist practices into his Tonghak doctrine and practices, perhaps to gain more converts for his cause (p. 26).[10]

Ch'oe, for example, suggested that altars should be built on mountain tops, especially on high mountains, in order to propitiate the spirits that bring fortune or misfortune. The worshiper had to learn "magic" formulas (some of which were combined from such characters as *kung*, *kung* and *ul*, *ul*) adapted from key words or ideographs taken from the *ch'amwisol* literature, which many Koreans believed had great efficacy for predicting national crises (p. 44).[11] In June 1861, Ch'oe is said to have come into possession of a kind of elixir, shaped like the characters *kung* and *ul* combined, and he formulated the twenty-one-letter incantation for immortality or longevity. In 1863, he widely propagated them to rid the evils from this world, along with his other instructions (pp. 44, 57).

According to Ch'oe, one "must drink a cup of water mixed with a sheet of paper" to become an immortal being (p. 78). One "must not eat bad meat of the four-legged animals [referring to dogs]"; one "should not suddenly jump into the cold [water in the] well for it is bad for health"; and one "should not recite the incantation in a high-pitched voice while lying [in bed]" (p. 46). In the process of obtaining immortality, one had to fall into a trance. In order to enter into a trance one had to go through a series of physical exercises in the form of singing songs, reciting incantations or poems, and doing ecstatic dances, practices which were not only prevalent but also inherent in shamanist religious ceremonies. Ch'oe also encouraged his followers to appreciate the aesthetic values of ballads, poetry, and music, some of which were equally valued in Confucianism, Buddhism, Taoism, Christianity, and Korean traditionalism (p. 103).

In the area of healing, one can also notice a synthesis of all existing ideas. Ch'oe accommodated Confucianism; to get elixirs and immortality one had to abide by the principles of sincerity *(song)* and respect *(kyong)*, without which he said one could not heal himself (p. 119). He admitted on several occasions that these two concepts came from Confucianism and that they were nothing but the results of human effort as found in it (p. 108). Also, he stated more than once that it is possible to cure disease without medication if one really has faith in and reverence for the Heavenly Master (pp. 35, 108). This gives us the impression that Ch'oe at this time seemed to think of healing in terms of its Christian counterpart.

In the method of childbearing, particularly of a male child, that was practiced by the Tonghaks, one also finds a synthesis of shamanism and other existing ideas. For example, Ch'oe used the concept of geomancy *(p'ungsu)*, a mixture of both Confucian and Taoist elements. He urged his followers to go to Kumkangsan (known as Mt. Diamond in Kangwon Province today) and select a place of residence in accordance with the principles of geomancy. Then they could bear not only male children but also highly gifted ones (pp. 110–11).

Equally interesting is the origin as well as the nature of Ch'oe's shamanism. Surprisingly, Ch'oe made no pretense of being original in this case. Explaining the origin of shaman, he said: "Han (Chinese) shamans came to our Eastern Region [referring to Korea] and spread their teachings to every household throughout the land." As to the nature of shamans, Ch'oe believed that everything, including heaven and earth, has and is a spirit or demon *(kwisin)*. In addition to this pantheistic and polytheistic view of shamanism, which in effect is characteristic of all primitive religions, Ch'oe further believed that his version of shamanism was the result of the interplay of the laws of geomancy, or *um* and *yang* (p. 116).

Here again, in discussing the theory and practice of shamanism, Ch'oe did not relate it in any way to the improvement of the state and society but regarded it only in a spiritual or religious way.

Lastly, let us examine the so-called Korean traditionalism in relationship to Ch'oe's Tonghak doctrine. According to Professor Yi Son-kun, in the Tonghak doctrine, "Confucianism, Buddhism and Taoism no longer function separately but in combination." This means that the human ethics of Confucianism, the spiritual awakening of Buddhism, and the Taoist detachment from the mundane world were integrated into the so-called Korean traditionalism. They had been developed by Ch'oe Ch'i-won, a noted reputable Confucian scholar of the Silla period, according to Yi. He expounded the three major Chinese ideas of Confucianism, Buddhism, and Taoism, and he synthesized them into a single system that became the foundation of the ideologies of the Hwarang elite, the ruling class of the Silla kingdom. According to Yi again, Ch'oe Ch'i-won is the direct ancestor of Ch'oe Che-u, that is, the latter is the twenty-eighth descendant of the former. On the basis of this family lineage, Yi concludes that Ch'oe Che-u inherited the Hwarang ideas and customs developed by his ancestor and integrated them into his own Tonghak doctrine.[12]

Although Yi's argument is somewhat controversial, a link seems to exist in terms of the similarities of custom and practice between the ninth century (the time of Ch'oe Ch'i-won) and the nineteenth century (the time of Ch'oe Che-u), at least in the area of nature appreciation, travel, and excursion. As has been pointed out earlier, Ch'oe Che-u was fond of traveling and visiting beautiful places such as rivers, lakes, mountains, and forests (pp. 43, 56, 97, 103–4, 106).[13] His love for nature is well demonstrated by his poetry, whose themes range from boats, flowers, bamboo, rivers, mountains, the moon, fish, and birds to sight-seeing (pp. 65–69). Among these things there is cogent, if not altogether convincing, evidence of similarities between the Tonghak and the Hwarang concepts of enjoyment or play *(yu)*. Both the Hwarangs and the Tonghaks traveled primarily in search of spiritual enlightenment, but they also traveled for the sake of enjoyment. This can be found in the words of Ch'oe Che-u: "Let us play and eat to the full" (p. 103).

But there is serious doubt about the validity of this interpretation. The fact is that Ch'oe compared himself to T'ao Yuan-ming, a famous Chinese poet who was noted for his love of nature, and also frequently quoted him in his writing (p. 39). In view of this conflicting evidence one cannot be dogmatic about the origin of the concept of play *(yu)*. Furthermore, it is difficult to equate the Tonghak doctrine and practice with the Hwarang counterparts, on the grounds that the former is more religiously oriented, whereas the latter is more militaristic and political on the whole. At best one can only say that a certain amount of so-called Korean traditionalism is blended, along with other ideas, into the Tonghak doctrine.

It is clear by now that the Tonghak doctrine as expounded by Ch'oe Che-u during the period 1860 to 1864 was not a single set of many separate ideas but a combination of many integrated and blended ideas. It was composed of existing Confucianism, Buddhism, Taoism, shamanism, and traditionalism, juxtaposed by and supplemented by the totally alien Christianity. In the course of Korea's long history, particularly from the first to the nineteenth centuries, many Chinese ideas came to Korea and then gradually became assimilated. This integration of Chinese ideas into Korea was so successful that Korean thinkers acquired the built-in habit of ideological or cultural syncretism to the extent that they no longer could distinguish one idea from the other. Nor were they conscious of the fact that their learning or culture was nothing but a syncretic form of ideas.

If there is anything new or unique in the synthesis of the Tonghak doctrine, it is that Ch'oe Che-u incorporated both the orthodox learning—Neo-Confucianism blended with Buddhism and Taoism—and the vulgar or heterodox ideas such as shamanism, traditionalism, and Christianity. Moreover, Ch'oe popularized both orthodox and unorthodox learnings, to the chagrin of the ruling elite, the patrons of orthodox learning.

In the period 1860 to 1864 the Tonghak doctrine took little or no interest in any political or social revolution. Instead it concerned itself with the reforming of the individual's mind and spirit, capitalizing more upon the existing yet acceptable ideas than upon the new. The Tonghak doctrine itself was apolitical. It taught its followers to resort to spiritual enlightenment in solving their political, economic, and social problems. It also appealed to them to reinforce the old order or ideas in order to succeed in their objective.

However, it is ironic that Ch'oe Che-u's Tonghak doctrine was branded as antigovernment and unacceptable to the ruling elite despite the fact that there was virtually no political content in the doctrine. If indeed Ch'oe had entertained any political ambition and incorporated it into his doctrine, he might and could have become a Hung Hsiu-ch'üan (of the Taiping Heavenly Kingdom) in Korea. Yet, unlike Hung in China, he did not use his doctrine for political advantage. Even when he was at the pinnacle of his prestige and influence, Ch'oe did not attempt to develop a political base in the politically and economically troubled society of Korea, which in many respects was comparable to that of China at about the same time. Equally ironic is the fact that after the sudden execution of Ch'oe in 1864 his followers found themselves and their interests drawn into the political and social arena against the initial wishes of their mentor, becoming political activists on the eve of the Sino-Japanese War of 1895.

NOTES

1. Chong-sik Lee, *The Politics of Korean Nationalism* (Berkeley, Calif., 1965), pp. 19–33. Also see Benjamin B. Weems, *Reform, Rebellion and the Heavenly Way* (Tucson, Ariz., 1964), p. ix. Lee has treated the Tonghak movement as a beginning of Korean nationalism, whereas Weems has regarded the Tonghak doctrine as "quasi-religious ideology" connected with political movements. The most recent work on the subject is James Kenneth Ash, "The Tonghak Rebellion: Problems and Interpretations," *Bulletin of the Korean Research Center* (June 1969), No. 30, pp. 89–106. In addition to these Western works there are a considerable number of articles on the subject written by both Korean and Japanese scholars. But they all have treated the subject more or less from the political, social, or economic standpoints. For further information

and bibliography, see Yi Ki-paek, *Hankuk sa sinron* (New interpretations on Korean history; Seoul, 1967), pp. 314–20.

2. Max Lerner, *Ideas Are Weapons* (New York, 1939), p. 8.

3. Karl Mannheim, *Ideology and Utopia: An Introduction to the Sociology of Knowledge* (New York, 1939), p. 50.

4. Weems, *Reform, Rebellion and the Heavenly Way*, pp. 7–12.

5. *Tongkyong taechon* (Great canon of Tonghak classics), ed. and trans. Ch'oe Tong-hwi (Seoul, 1961), pp. 15–16. This collection contains Ch'oe Che-u's writings such as poems, essays, and songs. The *Tongkyong taechon,* originally published in 1890, was used by Ch'oe Tong-hwi. The *Yongtam yusa* (Posthumous poems on Tonghak) is included at the end of this work. The *Yongtam yusa* and *Tongkyong taechon* are considered to be the basic canons of Tonghak. Hereafter *Tongkyong taechon* will be cited in the body of the paper by page number only.

6. Joseph H. Longford, *The Story of Korea* (New York, 1911), p. 14.

7. Weems, *Reform, Rebellion and the Heavenly Way,* p. 8.

8. James Legge, *The Sacred Books of China: The Text of Taoism* (New York, 1891), p. 47. According to Legge's translation of Tao, "The Tao that can be trodden is not the enduring and unchanging Tao. The name that can be named is not the enduring and unchanging name. (Conceived of as) having no name, it is the Originator of heaven and earth; (conceived of as) having a name, it is the Mother of all things."

9. Wing-tsit Chan, *A Source Book in Chinese Philosophy* (Princeton, N.J., 1963), pp. 271–96.

10. See also John Lofland, *Doomsday Cult* (Englewood Cliffs, N.J., 1966), especially pp. 1–4 and 14–28. This study points out startling similarities in the religious doctrines and practices of Ch'oe Che-u and Soon Sun Chang (rather, Chang Sun-son). Chang, a young Korean electrical engineer during the late 1940's and early 1950's, received a series of what he took to be messages from God, which he began to preach in the late fifties and early sixties in Korea and the United States. It is interesting to note that there are certain elements of shamanism in Chang's religious thinking and practice, as there were in Ch'oe's counterparts. These similarities may be due to the long history and great importance of shamanism among the Koreans.

11. See also Weems, *Reform, Rebellion and the Heavenly Way*, pp. 8, 19; Lee, *Politics of Korean Nationalism,* p. 28, Ash, "Tonghak Rebellion," pp. 92–93.

12. Yi Son-kun, *Hankuk sa hyontae pyon* (Contemporary Korean history; Seoul, 1963), p. 125.

13. About the concept of *yu* (play) as related to travel and nature appreciation and to the cultivation of the Hwarang elan, see Chong-sun Kim, "Hwarang and the First Unification of Korea" (Master's thesis, University of Washington, 1961).

The Language of Modern Hinduism: Cognitive Models and Ethnoscientific Analysis

A. Bharati
Syracuse University

When the founding fathers of anthropology, Tylor and Fraser, speculated on the origins of religion at a time when such questions were both permissible and in style, they overrated the cognitive function of religious systems at the cost of their orectic and affective elements. It was for this reason that they regarded primitive religion in the light of nineteenth-century intellectualism and evolutionism, which was the pervasive vogue of the day. Thus they gave good and bad marks, figuratively speaking, to religious practices reported to or read by them from whatever meager and undisciplined cross-cultural material they could find. For them, religion and magic were "pre-logic" or bad science or "pre-science" or whatever; and the notion held and shared by many later writers was that religion was bound to decay to the extent that science provided answers for unanswered questions. Had Tylor and Fraser, or even Durkheim and Weber, heard the astronauts read from Genesis as they cruised back to earth from the moon, they might have modified their contention.

I have come to the conclusion that three separate models have to be used for investigating the cognitive, the orectic, and the affective patterns of religious behavior. For the orectic or conative, decision models such as recently suggested by Izmirlian should be in order;[1] for the affective patterns, some psychiatric models might be useful—I am thinking particularly of the Ganser syndrome.[2] For the cognitive patterns, however, I suggest that ethnoscience and ethnosemantics provide the most appropriate and certainly the most recent model. I shall be concerned only with the cognitive aspect of religion, using modern Hindu linguistic behavior as my paradigm. During the past few years I have used other models, derived specifically from contemporary ordinary language philosophy of the type propounded by British and American analytic philosophers such as J. L.

Austin, Stuart Hampshire, A. Louch, and others.[3] I do not think that ethnoscience supersedes the ordinary language-analysis approach, but it most certainly complements it. I very strongly feel that psychological frameworks such as those used by culture and personality anthropologists are quite futile when it comes to subtler points such as the apologetic forensics used by modern Hindus.[4] The naïve Freudian scales presupposed by Carstairs and the somewhat ludicrous reductionism of P. Spratt obfuscate the issues—they do not even state the issues, let alone clarify them.[5]

Long ago I became quite disillusioned with the time-honored approach of philological Orientalists to Asian religions. Some Indologists that I have known entertain astoundingly naïve views about practiced and about grass-roots Hinduism on the village level, much as they display amazing ignorance about Indian society even when they have spent many, many years in the midst of it. I know an eminent scholar who spent about thirteen years in Benares and is regarded highly by pandits and by his Western colleagues, including myself. Yet he tells me that "there is no corruption in India" and that "caste has been abolished," although "you cannot be hired unless you belong to the caste of the person who hires"—in other words, he accepts quite uncritically the nonsense presented to him by his neighbors in India and by the Indian press. The rude fact is that the Sanskrit, Pali, and Tibetan texts tell us little about contemporary Hinduism and Buddhism; and it was with some puzzlement that I came to realize that Indologists refuse to see what the freshman anthropology student learns in his first course—that doctrines taught by the tradition are but tenuously connected, where they are connected at all, with the practices, beliefs, and ritualistic procedures used by its practitioners. Of course—and I have heard this rejoinder quite often—the Indologist is really not interested in what people do; he is interested in the literary, in the philosophical, and in the "truth" factor involved in the teachings. If this is so, he should really renounce his claim to having a special status different from and higher than that of his colleagues in such better-known departments as Classics, English, and Romance Languages. To the more cynical anthropologist, the German-born professor of German in a German-language department at an American university is an informant about contemporary middle-class German culture, on the same plane as a village smith in Bavaria—what the professor of German tells us about the Germans is indeed *emic* information. In a somewhat perverse fashion, what the Indian or Occidental Indologist tells us about Indian culture and religion, in informant-stuff, is *emic* rather than *etic*. Therefore, I feel that the social scientist, who has created the *emic-etic* model of observation and analysis,[6] is more than one up on his Indological colleague, though anthropologists working in the Indian field often display a guilt and/or shame complex for not knowing any Sanskrit and not too much of a modern Indian language. I am satisfied, then, that the new ethnography, utilizing the *etic-emic* approach for its analyses and the more general ethnoscientific attitude toward the informant and toward the message that is given by the informant and is decoded by the anthropologist, can come to grips with some of the subtle, ideological problems that older ethnology could not handle. Of course, that was one of the reasons why older anthropology gave a wide berth to highly literate societies whose ritual and belief systems were closely bound up with the written lore.

In the period between the end of World War II and the late fifties, a sort of methodological interregnum occurred, when social scientists such as M. N. Srinivas, R. Redfield, and some of their students and colleagues at Chicago and elsewhere attempted to create a new approach through the "Great Tradition"–"Little Tradition" dialectic. That was fairly fruitful, but it really did not deliver the goods in the long run. I have suggested an improved version of the "Great-Little Traditions" approach with special reference to the Indian situation,[7] but I think that the ethnoscientific approach now available outdistances all the previous attempts from the standpoints of clarity and fertility. I believe, however, that for our special case—a contemporary religious system of India in its cognitive parameters—the ethnoscientific model has to be supplemented by what I call "cultural criticism."[8] This means the method of eliciting radical responses from subjects by *challenging* their previous statements about their own culture as not conforming to a superior standard accepted by the informant himself, or by scientific standards that he would endorse were he familiar with them. A very simple example: modern Indians complain about the corruption of officials, the scarcity of doctors and nurses, the lack of altruism, and so forth; and, of course, when the outsider criticizes these things, the friendlier among his Indian hosts will chime in. But you cannot criticize Mohandas Gandhi or Subhas Chandra Bose or the *Bhagavad-Gita* without risking a head-on collision, dialectically. But it is precisely this sort of confrontation that the anthropologist seeks when using my "cultural criticism" as an elicitative method. This is simple psychology of a nonacademic kind: if you make a man mad, he will tell you the truth, though he may regret it afterwards. The only real danger is that the researcher may lose his visa, or not get another one when he wants to come to India again; but this can happen for many other reasons.

The group that I shall now analyze consists of modern, literate Hindus. For all practical purposes, they are coextensive with the "Indian Intellectual" in the peculiar, but well-taken, denotation suggested by Edward N. Shils.[9] This term is semantically quite different from the contemporary American or European use of the term "intellectual," which has been studied discursively by Richard Hofstadter.[10] My recent work on the Indian intellectual qua apologist for modern Hinduism sums up many if not most of the problems involved in a sociological survey of the communicative problems involved in mapping Hinduism as it is today—not the grass-roots Hinduism of the villages, which is not my subject here, but the highly eclectic, alienated urban Hinduism.[11] Until I began studying this numerically infinitesimal, but operationally supremely important, style of Hinduism, no one in any of the feeder disciplines had really done any work on it. Indologists regard it beneath their dignity to speak about the latter-day saints and preachers of nineteenth- and twentieth-century Bengal, Maharashtra, and Madras, since none of them knew or wrote in Sanskrit; and anthropologists concentrate on "their village." But the Hinduism I am talking about is the belief system of the people who run India and are going to run it for a very long time to come; it is also the Hinduism of the Hindus who go to school in the West and of Hindu expatriates in all parts of the world; and lastly, it is the Hinduism that may very well become the dominant belief system in India, if the contemporary educational authorities succeed in generating the sort of ideological assent that they want to see in the school systems of modern India, on every educational level.

The late Richard Robinson suggested quite rightly that there are really two, and only two, approaches to complex cultural and ideological networks. Using a strategical model, you can surround and encircle your target and move in upon it from all sides—which of course would be ideal, but is not very feasible when humans and research resources are sparse and the target is large and complex; alternatively, you can use the "parachute-drop" method—you land whatever paratroopers you have in the known vicinity of the target and they then assemble close to it and accomplish their mission. When translated into our research, this implies that when personnel and research facilities are insufficient, random or not-quite-random topics, properly investigated, should provide a sample for more general patterns involved. In eliciting or inferring responses from informants or from cultural objects encountered, the investigator hopes to produce viable samples on the basis of the corpus of information generated by the live or the inanimate "informant"—including the cult-object, text, song, and so forth—as manipulated by the religious specialists or by the laity. The obvious shortcoming of this approach derives from what Malinowski referred to as the "standardisation of optimism," in a different though related context; we simply have to have a good hunch when we depend on the samples at hand, rejecting those that appear to us to be atypical.

We have dropped down onto religiously fertile soil, somewhere near Kashmere Gate in the residential-cum-business area of Old Delhi—but we might have dropped into similar areas in Lucknow, Kanpur, or Meerut; though we would find somewhat different things in Calcutta, Bombay, or Madras. I shall present six themes which are sufficiently typical to chart the Hinduism of the modern Indian of the urban middle class. First, how does the modern urban Hindu define a Hindu? Next, what are his written authorities? Third, who are his personal, living guides? Fourth, what is his homiletic, exegetical, and, more general, his interactional style in communicating or thinking about Hinduism? Fifth, what is his actual or conceived link to social reality? And, finally, which aspects of the tradition does he reject in the process of vindicating and legitimizing his own involvement with Hinduism?

In all these topics, I shall show the *emic* or *etic* status of varying or alternative descriptions.

What is a Hindu? The traditional answer is pretty clear, though we are all aware that the term "Hindu" itself is not old—certainly much more recent than the ideas that constituted the Hindu belief system at the time when the term "Hindu" was first used. Traditionally, a Hindu is a person born into a Hindu *jāti*, an actual caste; this alone suffices on all counts. Hinduism is of a sociological order, and—very different from all other extant literate religions—its ideological counterpart has never entered the minimal definition of a Hindu. However, when a traditionalist feels pressed to enlarge the sociological by an ideological definition, he would define a Hindu, in terms of his belief system, as a person born into a Hindu *jāti* who accepts the authority of the Veda (the *sruti* texts, that is) on a par with the other epistemological *pramāṇas*, or cognitive verification principles—that is, *pratyakṣa* (direct perception) and *anumāna* (correct syllogistic inference). This has to be added, even though only implicitly, in order to state the degree of "acceptance" of the Veda—for, of course, "acceptance" is a somewhat woolly, inclusive sememe unless it is narrowed down to a genuine one-to-one lexeme. Now the modern Hindu's definition is radically different: There may be many Hindus, particularly in the traditionally more sophisticated and conservative Dravidian South, who would tacitly assume the traditional definition, modifying it by adding some new emphases; but our modern Hindu in the North will not only not accept this sociological-ideological definition, he will tend to reject it quite emphatically. A Gujarati lady-doctor living in Delhi told me, when I asked her for her definition of a Hindu, that "every good person who believes in God" is a Hindu. Did that include Muslims, Christians, Jews, and so forth? Yes, it did, for Hinduism was "all-embracing." Did it include Buddhists and Jainas, whose doctrine is atheistic? There was some hesitation, but then she said: "Yes, it includes Buddhism and Jainism, for they also believed in God, although they did not say so." On several occasions after this note was taken (1955), I asked Hindus who had affinal kinship ties with Jainas, if they thought Jainas were Hindus, too. The answer was almost always affirmative, though the stress then seemed to shift to the sociological rather than the ideological segment of the definition; for Hindus and Jainas of the merchant castes intermarry freely. Jaina women bringing along their *kuladevatā* (tutelary household deities) and merging them with those of their Hindu husband, and vice versa. Committed Jainas, however, did not share this view and would say that Jainas and Hindus are very different indeed—they would tend to disregard the sociological parameter and stress the ideological contrast. Now the lady-doctor's view of what makes a

Hindu a Hindu was, of course, quite radically "modern"; it is not shared by most other modern Hindus. On the other end of an imagined continuum beginning with the definition that is least divergent from the traditional concept and ending with that which is most strongly opposed (the latter being represented by the view of the lady-doctor), there are many intermediary notions. In all of them, we can isolate different emphases of the sociological and the dialectical order, with a shift from sociological to ideological definitions toward the radical end of the continuum. "Everybody who believes in God and is a good man" is an *emic* statement of religious assignations, which identifies modern, literate, urban Hindus of northern India. Amazingly, no modern Hindu, unless he happens to be a pandit and a professional Sanskritist, would define a Hindu *etically* in the manner that I did earlier. I will not go into the psychological or historical etiology of this strange shift from a highly restricted definition of the term "Hindu" to what must appear to any student of religion to be an extremely unctuous, wishy-washy, and overly general type of eclectic inclusion. I would only say that this *emic* use of "Hindu" rests on the polemic inherent in reformed Indian religion; the pin-pointing, narrowing, highly structured definitions of the classical tradition are thought to be not only outmoded and socially dysfunctional, but positively immoral.

What are the written authorities to which the modern Hindu refers? In the first place, of course, the average informed layman among urban Hindus knows very much more about, and is much more highly motivated toward, theological quest than is the average non-Indian, urban, middle-class person in most other areas of the world, including Asia. Still, this does not mean that the modern Hindu has more than a fleeting idea about the texts. I would say that the average middle-class Hindu in North India has read the *Bhagavad-Gita* in a Hindi or English translation and has listened to some standard Vedic prayers and formulas. He may also know some vernacular religious songs of the *ḳirtan* and *bhajan* type, which are not scripture but are postmedieval creations; and he will, more often than not, hum a *filmi* version of these. I own a rather large copy of a Hindi book *Mirā bhajans to be sung to the tunes of Anārḳali and Mahal.*[12] With members of the Arya Samāj and its more involved sympathizers the situation is quite different—they despise the entire non-Vedic pattern by decree, as it were, having their own fundamentalist, highly formalized and simplified Vedic ritual, both domestic and congregational. But I am excluding the Arya Samāj and its membership from this study, even though they do form an important middle-class segment in some cities of the North. Since their handling of the tradition is aggressively predefined, as it were, and their belief and ritual systems highly structured, they are really atypical for our purpose, although their ideological style has diffused, to a very thorough degree, to non-Arya Hindu groups (*sanātani* being the North Indian term to distinguish them, meaning "eternal"—that is, conservative), especially in the Punjab and the adjacent urban areas of western Uttar Pradesh.

Our North Indian, urban, modern Hindus, then, regard the *Bhagavad-Gita* as the "Bible of Hinduism"—I enclose the expression in quotation marks, since it is an *emic* term in modern Hindi-English. Etically, of course, this is quite wrong, since the *Bhagavad-Gita* does not have canonical, or *sruti*, status; it belongs to the epic and has therefore only *smrti*, or noncanonical, conventional status. There are easily traceable historical reasons, for this, which I shall not go into here.[13] I must emphasize this contemporary perception of the *Gita*: it is the most quoted, the most often translated, and most easily accessible of all scriptures; it has been read widely outside India, and this fact is very well known. It was Gandhi's vade mecum, and even the pronounced secularists of the political and administrative echelons regard it and refer to it as the sacred guide to secular action. In fact, some important political and educational figures have identified "Hinduism," as a set of beliefs, with the content of the *Bhagavad-Gita*. Pandit Madan Mohan Malaviya, founder of the rightist and potentially fascist Hindu Mahasabha, used to say that a Hindu was a person who believed in rebirth and the *Bhagavad-Gita* and was a vegetarian.[14] This sentiment has been reiterated by at least one extremely wealthy and influential industrialist,[15] and it is somehow the ideological underpinning of the staff and the administration of Benares Hindu University, the most important "secular" institution of higher learning in Northern India, outside of Delhi. Now if you combine the *emic-etic* technique with that of cultural criticism, responses are acute and fertile. If you suggest to the subject that the *Bhagavad-Gita* is noncanonical, *smrti* rather than *sruti*, most informants will either deny the knowledge of such distinction—and, of course, this denial is quite sincere, as none but pandits know the distinction—or they will assert that the *Bhagavad-Gita* is the true *sruti*. Some of them may quote a famous self-eulogy of the *Gita*, a verse ascribed to Vyāsa, the legendary author of the epic: "All the Upanishads are the cows, Krishna is the cowherd . . . the *Gita* is the milk" *(sarvopanisado gāvo dogdhā gopālanandana)*. There are two alternative explanations: either the speakers do not understand the definitional status of *sruti* and *smrti* in terms of their relation to the belief system of the Hindu tradition; or they do understand it, however vaguely, but they reject the distinction systematically. I tend to believe that the latter alternative is the correct one. Several highly informed spokesmen for modern, urban Hinduism made it quite clear to me, independently of one another, that the distinction between *smrti* and *sruti* was out of place, wrong, outmoded, a "superstition" (about this important term and its use, see below). The obfuscation or eradication of the distinction is "systematic" in Russell's sense—that is, it is dialectically necessary for the purpose of legitimizing further statements—statements, that is, that encode the modern, urban Hindu belief system. To put this into the simplest and most uncircuitous form, the Upanishads and the Veda *samhita*—that is, the *sruti*—are quietistic; they stress *jñāna* (intuitive knowledge), which entails withdrawal from society, emphasizing the virtues of the recluse, and so forth. There is little or no *bhaḳti*[16] in those texts, no *ḳarma-yoga*[17] worth mentioning, and hence no social incentive. On the other hand, the *Bhagavad-Gita*, which is a soldier's pep talk to another soldier, etically speaking, generated all these values—heroism, intensive social activity and involvement, singlemindedness in secular pursuits, and so forth. At least this is how the modern Hindu, following Vivekananda and other interpreters of this century, sees it. More learned, conservative readings of the *Bhagavad-Gita* are simply not known; Shamkarācārya's *bhāsya* (commentary, about A.D. 800), which makes the *Gita* out to be a text that teaches withdrawal and contemplation, or Sri Aurobindo's commentary (1946), which reads it as a text for integral yoga, are known only to experts and have no operational influence on the modern Hindus modally selected.

Next to the *Bhagavad-Gita*, which tops the scriptures in the Hindu's mind, rank the medieval and modern texts, poetic and homiletic, which have been written and communicated by the agents of the Hindu Renaissance since about A.D. 1500—for example, the founders of the *bhaḳti* movements, including Sikhism, Kabir, Mirā, and others, and, more importantly, the writings of the latter-day English-speaking saints, the swamis *since* Vivekananda. I say "since" because he established a tradition the importance of which is vastly underrated for reasons that I have pointed out in my article on the Hindu Renaissance.[18] The swamis of the Ramakrishna Mission; the Aurobindo people; the Divine-Life Society around Sivananda; the Self-Realization League around Yogananda Paramahamsa; Sāi Baba; Meher Baba, Swami Chinmayananda; and, of course, Maharishi Mahesh Yogi, erstwhile guru of Mia Farrow and the Beatles—their sayings and writings, whatever their literary and exegetical merit, have scored total success with our audience. When modern Hindus speak about the *Bhagavad-Gita*, or the *Upanishads*, the great majority among them have some swami's exegesis in mind. Again, I am not talking about the Arya Samāj, with its large middle-class following in Northern India—their lore is certainly not the English "pony" used by the collegiate and subcollegiate swamis of the land, but that of Dayānanda Sarasvati, who did not know any English and was quite overtly hostile to English-language use.

This takes us smoothly into the third theme of our study of legitimation in modern urban Hinduism: the spoken word. By the spoken word we mean the word of the lay and monastic teachers who live in the cities and move between the cities. They carefully avoid the village, which is left to grass-roots practitioners, both monastic and sacerdotal. They also avoid, though apparently to a decreasing extent in the last decade, the rostrums of learned Brahmanical dispute and erudition, the *pandāl* of Brahmin and monastic scholars, and the traditional *sāstrārtha* (exegetical disputation), which has been and still is the vehicle of learned, Sanskrit-based dialogue and is highly exclusive and totally unregenerate from a modern, critical viewpoint.

The ramifications of modern oral lore and its sustenance are perfectly amazing and partly grotesque. Consider the modern religious "calendar art." As to the artistic merit of this type of artifact, there is virtually no debate. Let me only say that its demerits are simply not recognized, or are not acknowledged, by modern Hindus, with the exception of some modern art schools in Bombay and Calcutta, but *not* with the exception of university scholars, lawyers, and professionals. "A picture of God is a picture of God," a Delhi businessman told me; and that, I believe, wraps it up as a modal statement. These polychromes abound in every niche and nook in India and Southeast Asia and wherever there is a sizable number of Indian expatriates—I have seen them in dozens of Punjabi Sikh houses in British Columbia and California and in East Africa. Ainslie Embree, when he was a professor at Columbia University, once hung up half a dozen of these polychromes in his office, eliciting responses from visiting Indian graduate students and faculty over a period of three months. There was only one negative response, and that, as I found out later, was made by an Indian anthropologist who had heard me talk about these oleographs. He suggested that there was an Embree-Bharati imperialist conspiracy to downgrade Indian aesthetics. More important, however, for our purpose, are the doctrinaire implications so well displayed on the picture; modern Hinduism and its teachers are radically eclectic. This has to do, in a narrower context, with the systematic confusion between *sruti* and *smrti*, which feature is either part of the etiology or part of the consequence of that eclecticism. Personally, I feel that the *sruti-smrti* confusion is etiological; for once the *smrti* obtains a de facto equivalent status with the *sruti*, the much more rambling and eclectic assemblages of ideologized ritualistic and theological-mythological themes are automatically absorbed into the total corpus constituting the belief system. It would then appear quite natural that new elements, such as those derived through occidental contacts, could be amalgamated without trouble, particularly if some sort of indigenous mantle could be given to them.

On the syncretistic matrix underlying the whole system, the Swamis, following Vivekananda, have successfully established the notion that Hinduism is *tolerant*, that it does not reject any religion, that it is based on the truths contained in all the religions of the world, or, conversely, that all religions of the world are true since they derived their inspiration, in however distant a past, from India. The whole complex of total diffusion of all cultural and technical goods from Vedic India derives from this pattern: atomic weaponry and airplanes were known to the heroes of the *Ramayana* and the *Mahabharata*; the Germans made away with Vedic secrets, which Hitler then channeled into his victories; *Arjuna* went to Pātāla, hence that part of the world is called "Argentina"; and so on.[19] Statements made by highly erudite Indian scholars about the age of the Veda, the origin of the Aryans, and the impact of Indian ideas on other parts of the world have been highly embarrassing and frustrating to Occidental students of India, whose reaction has either been one of indignation or of sarcasm, or a mixture of both. I do not think that these ambiguous sentiments need to be nurtured in the light of the new ethnography. I suggest that all statements that express the modern Hindu belief system—for example, "India is spiritual, the West is materialistic"; "Hinduism is scientific"; "Hinduism is the oldest religion in the World"; "Every good person who believes in God is a Hindu"; "Every person who believes in rebirth, the *Bhagavad-Gita*, and purity of Mother Cow is a Hindu"; and so forth—are *emic* and as such are not further analyzable as to their "correctness." When we use an *emic* technique, we perform a better job as anthropologists, though not necessarily as philosophers. We can counter and refute these statements by *etic* devices—such as my own method of "cultural criticism"—telling any of these informants that what *they say* makes a person a Hindu simply doesn't make him one by the standards set by the people who formulated that part of the tradition to which they, the modern Hindus themselves, grant authority. But this means undercutting the anthropologists' intention to report faithfully cultural behavior as it is, not as it should be.

I think it can be shown that the chief agents of Neo-Hinduism are the sadhus, not the Brahmins nor the college teachers and writers on Hindu philosophy in English. Not all sadhus, however: the orthodox—or better, the "orthopractical"[20] sanyasins and other ordained members of highly hierarchical and specialized monastic orders—have a hold on the villager and on the grass-roots scholars. But there is very little more than a polite exchange between these monks and the train-and-plane-traveling jet-set sadhus who formulate Neo-Hinduism and whose audience, proportionately very small when compared to the grass-roots Hindus of the village and the shrine, nevertheless runs India. Pandit Nehru was extremely antagonistic toward the orthodox sadhus; he called them loafers, parasites, fissiparous individuals, and others things, in angry Indian English. But he gave high respect to the Ramakrishna Mission, and he saw Swami Nikhilananda of New York to the car outside the prime minister's residence in New Delhi. The Ramakrishna Mission has the full confidence of state governments; large sums are entrusted to it for famine relief, control of epidemics, and social work. This, of course, is due to the fact that Vivekananda Westernized his monastic order—there is little of the Hindu-

Buddhist monastic tradition in the Ramakrishna Order, and it is run, efficiently and smoothly, on the lines of Christian charitable missions; in fact, Vivekananda hardly denied this scheme. But when it comes to a showdown, the modern swamis are certainly not taken seriously by the agents of the grass-roots tradition. At the *kumbhamelā*[21] in Allahabad in 1954—where I had the honor of being appointed *sevak*[22] to his late Holiness Swami Bharati Krishna Tirtha, Samkarācārya of Govardhanapitha-Puri—two Ramakrishna Mission swamis from the Allahabad Center wanted to join the *akhārā*[23] for the procession and the ritualistic dip in the holy river, the highlight of the occasion. They were refused admission into the *akhārā* and were told to take their dip afterwards with the lay pilgrims, who numbered roughly a quarter million. "These people," a senior monk of the Dasanāmi Order told me later in his tent, "pick up the excrements of the sick and carry leather briefcases, and wear stitched shirts—why don't they join the government? Why do they pretend to be sadhus?"

The fact is that modern Hindus take their ideological cue from the swamis who "pick up the excrements of the sick," literally or metaphorically, and who espouse social service, and so forth, declaring Hinduism to be a religion that is both "scientific" and humanitarian. This, incidentally, accounts for the wrath that anthropologists encounter from modern Hindus when they study and report grass-roots Hinduism, which is summarily rejected as "superstition" by modern urbanites.

As a participating observer, you can watch a modern swami perform. Swami Chinmayananda's *jñāna-yajña* is something that has to be seen to be believed. These "wisdom-sacrifices" in the large cities of India assemble ranking political and business leaders in town, with civil servants of all grades. There is a lot of social display, and classical terminology is used for denoting very modern activities. I wanted to see the swami somewhere, as I happened to be visiting the place where he was conducting his *yajña*. "His Holiness has gone for *bhiksā*," a devotee told me. *Bhiksā*, of course, is the process of going the rounds to obtain food by begging. As it happened, he was having lunch with the governor of the state at the latter's palatial mansion; the devotee knew this, but then *bhiksā* is an *emic* term for *any* food that *any* sadhu takes *any*where.

Philip Singer calls this process "*sadhuization*,"[24] a term emendatory to "Sanskritization," "Hinduization," "Parochialization," "Westernization," and so forth—terms that have been in vogue among anthropologists writing about religious behavior in South Asia. He claims, quite rightly I believe, that the sadhu is not really a charismatic in Weber's sense; in fact, I would say charisma as we understand it has no *emic* equivalent in India. A sadhu is a saint by ascription, quite without regard to his personal powers, his attraction, or his learning. By ascription he has the eight great *siddhis*;[25] he is in the state of *samādhi*[26] or any of its equivalents at all times; he needs no proof of his powers—there is no possible way to disprove them, since nothing he does, or fails to do, can repudiate his ascribed status. The only condition is that he have an audience, and it is this which decides whether people will refer to him as a saint or as a fraud. This being so, the term "saint" (North Indian *sant*) is a descriptive term, contrasting with the evaluative use of "saint" in European languages. A person who is ordained in any order or who lives a full-time religious career can and will introduce himself as "Saint So-and-so," and there will be no smiles and no frowns in a North Indian audience.

The ritual conducted by the sadhus is not Vedic, nor does it really fit any formalized standards; it is largely of the *ḳirtan-bhajan-ḳathā* variety,[27] with formal lectures over electronic sound systems becoming more and more frequent. From the highly literate type of *ḳirtan* described by Singer[28] to the occasional *bhajan* party at the house of some "householder" (*grhastha*—a technical Sanskrit word which has become a common vocable in the urban Hindu Renaissance), there is a wide range of performances of this informal type of ritual. This is in contrast to the formalized Vedic and other Sanskrit ritual, which, except for Arya Samāj practices, is thought to be reactionary and basically undesirable.

This takes us to the problems that anthropological jargon has circumscribed as processes of "Sanskritization";[29] quite briefly, the term connotes ritualistic and pararitualistic activities that tend to absorb bookish, ultimately Sanskrit-based ceremony and that utilize Brahmanical lore and Brahmin personnel for the performance in question. It does *not* mean the learning of Sanskrit or the use of Sanskrit for religious dialogue —quite the contrary, "Sanskritized" persons or social groups often denigrate the importance of Sanskrit as being reactionary and antimodernistic and as perpetuating the old order from which India should desist and separate. The term "Sanskritization" properly applies to rural and tribal communities rather than to urban groups—tribes and low-caste rural groups invariably "Sanskritize" their ritual and their way of life (by abandoning the eating of meat, by the remarrying of widows, and by certain other "non-Sanskritic" acts and customs) with the sole object of improving their lot and their social status. One might assume that the urban groups in question are situated at the upper end of the "Sanskritization" process, where different options and newer loyalties are available, including the modern media, formal education, and so forth.

The modern English-speaking sadhu is, in a somewhat paradoxical fashion, the agent of Sanskritization in spite of the fact that most modern sadhus do not know Sanskrit, although most of them pretend that they do. They can get away with it in the cities, so long as they operate within their middle-class, service- and trade-centered audiences. As was noted above, they avoid the holy places as well as the top-level grass-roots monastics, whose Sanskrit erudition is a known fact, but who are tagged as old-fashioned, reactionary, or even "superstitious," as we shall presently see, partly due to their stress on the homiletic and exegetical use of Sanskrit. Middle-class women in Delhi chant OM and learn two or three verses from the Sanskrit scriptures by heart—a thing that used to be totally unthinkable and still is in the more orthopractical regions of high-caste Hindu India: no woman is supposed to pronounce OM or chant Vedic texts, since by traditional definition any woman, even a Brahmin lady, is "like a *sūdra*"; she has no *samskāras*, that is, initiations entitling her to the ritualistic use of the Vedic lore.

However, unbeknown to the creators of Sanskritization terminology, the modern urban Hindus in northern India really fit eminently well into the stipulations of this terminology. Though they are more or less hostile to Sanskrit, they tend to toe the Sanskritic line—they tend to abandon meat-eating entirely or they confine it to minimal, clandestine consumption. Even Sikhs, known for their gusto for meat dishes, tend to become vegetarians under the ubiquitous influence of urban Hinduism. This sometimes operates via economic success: I have observed four cases, three in India and one in East Africa, where a Sikh became extremely wealthy and ceased to eat meat after some time. Women in urban Hindu caste-society seldom ate meat anyway, but before the emergence of what we could call Renaissance Power, or "swami power," eating only vegetarian food and reading or listening to the *Ramayana* and other texts in Hindi was felt to be for the ladies. This is bound to change quite rapidly now. It will result from the pull of the new eclectic Hinduism; but also the fact that schoolchildren in northern India learn highly Sanskritized Hindi at school will mean that they can now teach their parents, as it were, to understand the Hindi newscasts and that they can transmit a highly neologistic Sanskritized idiom to their fathers, who, until independence, preferred Urdu and Persian to Hindi and Sanskrit, leaving the latter two to the women about the house. Urdu, which used to be the hallmark of the middle-class urban North-Indian Hindu, is losing to this two-pronged attack—men over forty still read Ghalib and drool when they hear Urdu *ghazals*; their sons and daughters shrug it off, and the speech form that their fathers used is now being regarded as an idiolect and is doomed to become defunct in another generation.

Finally, I would like to select a single term to illustrate the parlance of modern urban Hinduism. I have treated this specific term in a separate publication,[30] but let me summarize my point and emend it for the purpose of accumulating material for the study of religious epistemology. The term "superstition" as used by modern urban Hindus is an *emic* term; it does not have the English dictionary meaning at all, and whatever lexico-semantic overlap there is, is of a trivial sort and does not in any way weaken my argument. Modern Hindus use "superstition" to denote, primarily, any activity, attitude, or thought pattern that is traditional and that is allegedly impervious to the postulates of modernization. This does, in a marginal fashion, include *etically* superstitious acts—except, of course, that we have to be careful about "superstition" in general, for it seems to me that this term, like "mental illness," is always *emic*; and if I were to elaborate my basic cynicism in these matters, I would posit that "superstition" really means any belief system that the speaker does not approve of, provided that it is tied to a culturally postulated extrahuman agency. However, in our specific case the term is applied to the official line of action and ideology, to secularism as propounded by the Indian leadership, to a deritualized, Protestant-ethic-directed cognitive religion of the eclectic sort as discussed earlier in this chapter, and to deemphasis on sectarian and primary-source-related theological argument. In practice, this means that the highly Sanskritic daily *pūjā* of the *engagé* Brahmins—all temple ritual, but also the persistence of dowry, of expensive wedding feasts, and the emphasis on any ritual-linked divinity and its service—are "superstitions." The only exception seems to be astrology, which is accepted and consulted as "scientific" by virtually all Indians, not just Hindus. Now, there is a fine exercise for the ethnosemanticist: What Indian term is translated as "superstition" by speakers of the modern Hindu Renaissance? None. Just like certain other phrases, which are *emic* Indian English, "superstition" as used by these speakers does not really translate any Indian term, hence they would use the English term even as they speak in a vernacular. Swami Dayānanda Sarasvati, the founder of the Arya Samāj, used a Sanskritic neologism not in vogue in Hindi before his time (around 1870–1880): that word is *andhavisvās*, literally "blind faith"; but here, as is almost always the case in the experience of the anthropologist, the etymology of a word, or of a phrase, is not only irrelevant but is highly obfuscating. The English usage of "blind faith" does not cover anything denoted by *andhavisvās*. Since Dayānanda, the word has come into vogue among Hindus, with its core reference being that of unreformed, unenlightened, traditional-ritualistic behavior without concern for social improvement. Now the term is used in a way that philosophical analysis calls a "recommendatory" use, and this use is wider than the "persuasive" use suggested by Charles Stevenson.[31] When a modern Hindu who knows English calls a type of thought or action *andhavisvās*, he has the literal meaning of "blind faith" in mind. When he then refers to such actions as daily domestic ritual, Sanskrit rote learning and recitation, and also processes of supernatural curing, soothsaying, and witchcraft as *andhavisvās*—literally "blind faith"—he thereby *recommends* that these things be thought of as superstitions. If he does not know English, then the pattern of expression follows the line set by the nineteenth-century reformers, who wrote and preached in the vernacular, particularly Swami Dayānanda. Since *andhavisvās* was a vernacular neologism using two Sanskrit morphemes that had never been compounded before, the meaning that Swami Dayānanda gave to this new compound has become the meaning now current in North Indian languages. Because it is a term of recent origin, there is little semantic ambiguity in its use, since there has not been enough time to aggregate new sememes to the lexical compound. We probably have here a very clear case of the Whorff-Sapirian syndrome—words preceding concepts: *andhavisvās* was not a "state of mind" or a type of action until reformers and their votaries pointed it out by generating a neologism that would specify an attitude that was to be condemned.

Let me briefly summarize the main conclusions of this investigation: urban, modern Hinduism has little to do with the two types of grass-roots Hinduism with which anthropologists have so far concerned themselves—it is not the "little tradition," the local ritual and belief system of the villages, with regional deities assuming all-Indian pantheonic features; nor is it the learned, scholastic Hinduism of the pandits and the orthodox sadhus. It is the highly eclectic brand of reformist pamphleteering, combined with the world view held and propagated by certain sermonizers around the turn of the century, particularly Vivekananda and, a bit earlier, Dayānanda Sarasvati. This urban Neo-Hinduism denigrates ritual of the traditional kind and rejects the scholastic subtleties of traditional theological dispute. It incorporates much of the Christian missionaries' teachings from around the turn of the century, without being conscious of this fact; and it regards the modern sadhu as a religious cynosure. On the ideological side, it rejects the quietistic, contemplative, recluse-oriented themes of the canonical texts and replaces them with selective noncanonical passages and texts that seem to stress social engagement and action. And finally, in order to solidify these radical deviations from the grass-roots tradition, it uses processes of partly conscious dissimulation, such as blurring the distinction between *sruti* and *smrti* (canonical and noncanonical texts) and by using pejorative neologisms, in a recommendatory fashion, to attack traditional grass-roots modes of religious belief and ritual systems.

NOTES

1. Harry Izmirlian, Jr., 'Structural and Decision-Making Models: A Political Example," *American Anthropologist*, 71.6:1062–74 (Dec. 1969).

2. The Ganser syndrome is well known in psychiatry: a person pretends to be insane—and when he persists, he actually develops psychopathological symptoms. This is one version; a more sophisticated reading, as given by Prof. Th. Szasz and Dr. R. Leifer, holds that the distinction should not be made in the first place, for the distinction between "being insane" and "acting insane" is linguistic, not substantive.

3. See A. L. Louch, *Explanation and Human Action* (Berkeley & Los Angeles, 1967).

4. I am thinking specifically of John J. Honigmann, Anthony F. Wallace, and Victor E. Barnouw—all three of whom have written texts entitled *Culture and Personality*. Prof. Francis Hsu calls this approach *Psychological Anthropology* (he edited an anthology with this title, published by Dorsey Press, Inc., 1961).

5. G. M. C. Carstairs, *The Twice Born* (Bloomington, Ind., 1958); Philip Spratt, *Hindu Personality and Culture* (Bombay, 1966). See also my reviews of this book in *Journal of Asian Studies*, 26:519–20 (May 1970), and in *American Anthropologist*, Feb. 1968, p. 142.

6. The use of the *etic-emic* model belongs to what Marvin Harris calls the "new ethnography." The terminology was created by Kenneth Pike, for of course it is a linguistic model in the first place. Though somewhat opposed by other ethnoscientists and ethnosemanticists, Harris's definitions of the *etic* and the *emic* are perfectly sufficient for our purpose: "Emic statements refer to logico-empirical systems whose phenomenal distinctions or "things" are built up out of contrasts and discriminations significant, meaningful, real, accurate, or in some other fashion regarded as appropriate by the *actors themselves* [i.e., by the native subjects we are talking about; italics supplied]. An emic statement can be falsified if it can be shown that it contradicts the cognitive calculus by which relevant actors judge that entities are similar or different, real, meaningful, significant, or in some other sense 'appropriate' or 'acceptable' " (Marvin Harris, *The Rise of Anthropological Theory* [New York, 1968], p. 571). "Etic statements depend upon phenomenal distinctions judged appropriate by the community of scientific observers. Etic statements cannot be falsified if they do not conform to the actor's notion of what is significant, real, meaningful, or appropriate. Etic statements are verified when independent observers using similar operations agree that a given event has occurred. An ethnography carried out according to etic principles is thus a corpus of predictions about the behavior of classes of people" (*ibid.*, p. 575).

7. A. Bharati, "Great Tradition and Little Traditions: An Anthropological Approach to the Study of Some Asian Cultures," in *Anthropology and Adult Education*, ed. Th. Cummings (Boston, 1968), pp. 72–94.

8. See A. Bharati, "Cultural Criticism as a Tool for Social Studies," *Quest* (Bombay), 33:15–22 (1962).

9. Edward N. Shils, *The Intellectual between Tradition and Modernity: The Indian Situation* (The Hague, 1961).

10. Richard Hofstadter, *Anti-intellectualism in American Life*, Vintage Books Vol. 317 (New York, 1966), pp. 18 ff.

11. A. Bharati, "The Hindu Renaissance and Its Apologetic Patterns," *Journal of Asian Studies*, 29.2:267–89 (Feb. 1970).

12. *Anārkalī* and *Mahal* were two of the most popular Hindi movies in the fifties; the songs, numbering roughly a dozen, have been sung and whistled by nostalgic males both in India and among Indian emigrants on all continents ever since.

13. But see this author's chapter, "Gandhi's Interpretation of the *Bhagavadgītā*," in *Gandhi: The Man and His Work*, ed. S. N. Ray (Philadelphia, 1970).

14. Transcript of a speech delivered by Malaviya at the convocation of Benares Hindu University in 1935.

15. Jugal Kishore Birla, eldest of the Birla brothers, now deceased.

16. *Bhakti* is the technical term for devotion to a personally conceived god; it is also the name of all schools and religious systems in India that base their teachings on personalistic devotion rather than on abstract, monistic concepts like those of the nondualistic Vedanta.

17. In this form, the term *karma-yoga* first appears in the *Bhagavad-Gita*. However, its semantic implications today derive from the writings of Swami Vivekananda, who created the notion of four yogas—namely, *karma-yoga*, "'yoga of selfless action"; *bhakti-yoga*, "yoga of devotion"; *jñāna-yoga*, "yoga of pure contemplation"; and *rāja-yoga*, or yoga of a psychoexperimental sort involving the concept of the *kundalini* (the coiled) power culled from *hatha-yoga* and other texts. The amazing thing is that very few people in India today, including good scholars, seem to be aware of the fact that no such arrangement was listed before Vivekananda. Furthermore, the term *rāja-yoga*, a misnomer due to Vivekananda, did not mean what Vivekananda said it did and what modern Hindus, following him quite uncritically, think it did. The psychoexperimental processes that Vivekananda was referring to are called *laya-yoga* in the traditional learned terminology, i.e., the "yoga of merging."

18. Bharati, "The Hindu Renaissance."

19. I heard this first from Sohan Singh, a Sikh *havildār* (sergeant) in the National Army during World War II. From a much more potent platform, I heard it again from Swami Anand at the *kumbhamelā* (all-Indian monastic and lay assembly) at Allahabad in 1954, in an audience that numbered about 200,000. See my article "Hindu Scholars, Germany, and the Third Reich," *Quest* (Bombay), Jan.–Mar. 1965, pp. 74–77.

20. This term was suggested, very felicitously, by Prof. J. A. B. van Buitenen in "On the Archaism of the *Bhāgavata Purāna*," in *Krishna: Myths, Rites and Attitudes*, ed. Milton Singer (Honolulu, 1966), p. 30.

21. The *khumblamelā* takes place at three different locations in northern and western India every twelfth year, when Jupiter, Saturn, and Neptune enter Aquarius. I have discussed the function and the importance of the *kumbhamelā* in another publication, q.v. "Pilgrimage Sites and Indian Civilization," in *Chapters in Indian Civilization*, ed. Joseph W. Elder, Vol. 1, *Classical and Medieval Period* (Madison, Wis., 1967), pp. 95 ff.

22. Literally, *sevak* means "servant"—the assistant of a monastic head during any public function, such as the *kumbhamelā*.

23. An *akhārā* (Hindi) is, literally, a gymnasium, a place for organized physical training among monks and novices. After the consolidation of Muslim rule, these athletic institutions gradually incorporated all the monastic institutions represented at the *kumbhamelās*, since they gave protection to the monks and since they also organized the monks into distinctive groups for the processions.

24. Philip Singer, "Sadhus and Charisma" (Ph.D. diss., Syracuse University, 1961).

25. Seven or eight occult powers are enumerated in the texts: powers such as *anima* (becoming as heavy as the earth), *laghimā* (becoming excessively light), *kāmatvam* (having all one's desire spontaneously fulfilled), *vaśīkarana* (getting into one's power—i.e., bewitchment, especially of women for sexual purposes, appearing at various places at the same time, traveling at enormous speed, etc.).

26. *Samādhi* literally means "bringing into one"—the consummative

mystical experience, incorrectly and far too generally referred to as "trance" by psychologists and anthropologists who are not conversant with the highly structured and skilled yogic situation.

27. *Kirtan* and *bhajan* are virtually synonyms, meaning litany and religious songs, solo or in chorus, with one leader and the lay audiences responding with the refrain, etc. *Kathā* (story) is the telling of mythological stories with a moral, an informal sermon on the basis of a mythological tale.

28. M. Singer, "The Radha-Krishna Bhajanas of Madras City," in *Krishna*, ed. M. Singer (see note 22, pp. 90–139).

29. The terms have been used diffusely by M. N. Srinivas, McKim Marriott, Milton Singer, myself, and many others. A critical assessment, very important in this specific context, can be found in J. F. Staal, "Sanskrit and Sanskritization," *Journal of Asian Studies*, 22:261–75 (1963).

30. See A. Bharati, "The Use of Superstition As an Anti-Traditional Device in Urban Hinduism," in *Contributions to Indian Sociology* (New Series), ed. T. N. Madan (Delhi, 1970).

31. Charles Stevenson, *Ethics and Language* (New Haven, Conn., 1958).

3

Distillations of Fermentation

EDITORIAL NOTE

How Shall We Model the World?

Robert J. Miller
University of Wisconsin

By and large, contemporary social scientists accept the idea of religion as a category equivalent to politics, economics, and social life—all "parts" of a greater whole, Society or its Culture. It becomes difficult, then, to discuss religious ferment in a context in which the categories refuse to be clarified even for purposes of analysis.

In this section our essayists have begun to move away from the rigidity of such analytic categories. Concerned with a process or processes, they have brought under consideration the old Asian tendency to view religion as life, or religion as coterminous with economics, politics, and social relationships. In short, the following papers search for new perspectives on religious ferment, following the processes that transform ideas into action. At times, in standard rubrics, an author seems to be dealing with the politicalization of religion. Again, some essays seek to emphasize the end product of religious ferment, stressing the mode in which religious values or ethics are transformed into imperatives for daily living: religion persists, but ferment is muted. Together with such a perspective, the model for the world is reaffirmed or reformulated in traditional religious terms. In fact, these papers suggest the beginning of the development of an analytical model of religious ferment in Asia or in other parts of the world.

Let us assume that what we are really dealing with is the problem of alternative models of system organization for attaining certain goals. It has often been claimed that the secularizing model is the wave of the future, while religious models are anachronistic, feudalistic, or unrealistic. Measure such models against a new, scientific world view, which emphasizes relative morality, relative goodness, and varying perspectives of reality. From this standpoint, religious models do tend to be anachronisms, dealing with truths, absolutes, apparently static social orders, and with avowed and to-be-accepted guardians of public conduct and thought. Religious ferment, in such cases, involves a reappraisal of their traditions by the guardians themselves, often reacting to the pressures of the populace they are guarding. If we recognize that for many of the guardians and the guarded the model needs only reconsideration and minor alteration—not *replacement*—in order to make it work more adequately, we can better understand the nature of this ferment. The question Ainslee Embree asks in his essay is indeed one that is not often asked: Why should the guardians of tradition cooperate in its destruction?

Whether we deal with fundamental *human* rights or with the *benefices of deities* and their human channels of communication, all such questions concern *sanctions for action.* At one level, the conflict of models is a conflict between those who seek to strengthen such sanctions by allocating them to the *religieux* for interpretation and those who claim the right to redefine the goals and the boundaries of existence by consensus. In both cases, imperatives of an ideological nature must inform human action. In all cases, there are appeals to greater goods, morality, or rights, which somehow transcend sheer individual, personal survival. Neither the religious traditionalists nor the secularizers and modernizers accept a simple existential view of the universe or the world they wish to construct.

Particularly at the level of organizations, groups, and movements, much ferment in religion shares with political ferment the agitation over legitimacy of control. In bald terms, shall the state or the dominant religious organization formulate the model of the world? Adherents to the model of secularizing states attempt to relegate religion (and its organized advocates) to a noncompetitive position. They stress that specific religious ideas are relevant to the *individual's* goals, but that, for utility, the *social* goals must eliminate sectarian content. Thus we return to the contrast between ethics and religion with which this volume began. Yet it is apparent that even in the most secular of states, religious organizations pose the threat of alternative models for belief and action. The state perforce must seek control or *use* of those organizations proposing the alternative models. In the process, the religious traditionalists reappraise the model to find ways of equating old imperatives with new demands: tradition is newly perceived, and the equations between old and new can be validated. Does this preserve the Temple or lead to its destruction?

Some of our essays suggest paradoxically that *preservation* is the end point of religious ferment. Yet if we momentarily revert to the analogy of fermentation to produce wines, there is a lesser paradox. If, at some point, fermentation does not stop, the product deteriorates from the desired peak. If any fermentation continues, it may take the form of slow, imperceptible change. Pressing the analogy, in our essays the "quiet ferment which absorbs the new into itself" may give the appearance of the stabilized brew. The natural ferment of ideas may be continuing, but translation of those ideas into the ferment of action may not yet have occurred, or it may have been controlled to preserve the product. In such a case as the Lamaists of West Bengal, preservation of a model of the world—preservation of the stability of a religious way of life (rather than of a religion per se)—mutes the effects of the ferment occurring around them. It would be a mistake, however, to see such populations as static or unresponsive to the agitation of the mind. The Lamaists (and similar populations in Asia) are entities in themselves from *their* point of view, but are parts of a much larger and more complex society when viewed from the outside. They are politically, economically, and socially articulated to the larger society, but *emotionally* they stand apart. For all such *encapsulated* part societies—societies *living* a model of the world not consonant with that of the dominant political-ideological system that surrounds them—ferment, quiet or unquiet, is a part of the daily life. For many of the groups, organizations, and societies discussed in this section, ferment has become a *component* of their system.

The Social Role of Religion in Contemporary India

Ainslie T. Embree
Columbia University

A modest indication of the contents of this paper would need a lengthy subtitle: "An impressionistic statement of the activities of some religious groups in selected areas of North India." And to this must be added an immediate disclaimer: there will be no references, except in the most oblique way, to the relation of religious ideologies to economic development.[1] Instead, for reasons I shall try to make clear, I shall focus on areas of tension and conflict where a religious vocabulary is used to articulate the aims and aspirations of the participants.

That the sources of information available for making a comment on the religious situation in modern India are so astonishingly meager is immediately relevant. Modern Indian religion has not received much scholarly attention in the West. Farquhar's great study has long been outdated, but it has never been replaced by a survey of the same caliber.[2] In India itself there are few scholarly journals and reviews dealing with contemporary religious phenomena,[3] and in the daily press, religion is almost always bad news. Communal riots; the support of untouchability by the Sankaracharya of Puri; the killings in Kashmir that followed the theft of the Prophet's hair; stories of human sacrifice at the laying of the foundations for a bridge in Rajasthan—these are the religious images that emerge from the Indian press.

Many thoughtful Indians, by no means personally ill-disposed to religious values and customs, have been led by such phenomena to conclude that the only creative role religion can play in India is to accept a self-denying ordinance—to remove itself from the political arena, where its intrusion serves only to hinder the search for social justice. A. B. Shah, one of the most interesting of Indian social critics, recently argued in this fashion quite explicitly: "India has enough problems to tackle apart from those created by the obscurantism of its communal parties and quasi-political groups; if religion is allowed to complicate these problems, we may as well give up all hope of creating a modern, secular democracy and a single nation out of the diverse groups constituting the people of India."[4] This is not a new note in Indian political thought; it echoes the criticism that such very different thinkers as Rabindranath Tagore and M. N. Roy made about the direction in which Gandhi led the nationalist movement.[5] Yet surely Gandhi's assessment—partly intuitive, partly the result of shrewd social analysis—that Indian nationalism would have to be articulated in a religious vocabulary was more realistic than that of his critics. Those who pleaded for a strictly political vocabulary may have been on the side of the angels of rationality, but they were asking Indian society to be other than what it is. This is not to suggest that Indian society is in some sense peculiarly spiritual or religious in contrast to other societies, but only that the vocabulary of political and social discourse in India in the modern period has been inextricably related to what, for lack of a better phrase, must be termed religious concerns. In this reality is rooted the response of the dominant religious forces in India to the political groups that are attempting to bring about rapid social change.

The conflict and tensions produced as religious formulations of society confront the agents of change have often been presented as the result of a headlong clash between the forces of tradition (or reaction) and those of modernity (or progress). Gunnar Myrdal, for example, has spoken of such a clash as a major motif of the unfolding Asian drama. One sees, he suggests, "a set of inner conflicts operating on people's minds: between their high-pitched aspirations and the bitter experience of a harsh reality; between the desire for change and improvement and mental reservations and inhibitions about accepting the consequences and paying the price."[6] This almost mythic vision is no doubt valid; but one should not assume that it takes the form of a collision between the defenders of traditional religion and the exponents of modernity. What is happening in India is, I would suggest, something much more complicated and more subtle.

As a basis for considering this conflict and tension, I would like to make three general observations. First of all, the spokesmen for traditional religious values are not merely defending the past, nor are they reactionary in any simplistic sense. They are, on the other hand, profoundly radical; for they, quite as much as the modernizers, have a vision of the future they intend to work for. The defenders of tradition are "modern men," quite as modern in their education, their life styles, and certainly in their political techniques as those who identify themselves with programs of change and modernization in politics and society. They have their own program of change and a blueprint of the good society, however fantastic it may seem to those who do not share their premises and their concerns. Second, in advancing their programs of change, the religious groups do not come in conflict so directly or so importantly with the agents of modernity as they do with other religious groups who have competing, or alternative, visions of the good society based on other perceptions of reality. As I will try to suggest, this fact explains both the ferocity and the increasing frequency of communal riots. And third, it seems obvious that those who care most deeply for traditional religious formulations—or, to put it another way, those whose personal identities are dependent upon such formulations—are most unlikely to cooperate in furthering the social and religious change desired by the modernizers. There has always been a curious ambivalence in the thinking of the modernizers on this point. Nehru at one time would speak of those who supported traditional religious life styles as obscurantists; at another, he would appeal for their cooperation in instituting a new social order. The modernizers never seem to ask themselves: Why should the guardians of tradition cooperate in its destruction? Perhaps one can summarize these three points by saying that the traditionalists—or the radical right, to use a more meaningful term—are not the debris of a retreating sea of faith, but are as much a part of the wave of the future as are the spokesmen for modernity.

The goals of the traditionalists can perhaps be most clearly perceived in relation to the aims of the modernizers. In reacting to the modernizers, the traditionalists tend to formulate their own view of the good society. The attitudinal changes desired, and the social and political forms for institutionalizing them, can be fairly summed up under four headings: national unity, social justice, political democracy, and secularism. These are the commonplaces of political rhetoric, of the five-year plans, of the Constitution itself. There is no need to spell out the specific content of these goals—except to say they all entail profound changes in the fabric of Indian society. Karl Marx was premature when he allocated to the British the credit for causing the only social revolution ever known in Asia by undermining the traditional society, which "had restrained the human mind into the smallest possible compass, making it the unresisting tool of superstition, enslaving it beneath traditional rules, depriving it of grandeur and historical energies."[7] It is only in our own time that this process seems to be really under way, with its agents coming from within the society itself. Each of the goals relates immediately to the interests of the articulate spokesmen for religion, because, as already stressed, they too have their vision for the future. It is perhaps fair to say that what may be defined as the spokesmen for the dominant political culture of India at the present time—the groups who hold actual political power, the heirs of the Indian National Congress even though many have long since gone into one form or another of opposition—are in agreement with regard to the importance of these goals, although not with regard to the mode of implementing them. It is when one turns to the other side of the equation—the traditional systems of life and thought—that the sources of tension become manifest.

There is no need to stress the fact that since Indian religious systems are not monolithic, it is impossible to make any generalizations about their responses to social change that cannot be easily challenged. Even more than with most systems of belief, those of India display an internal fragmentation that is derived from geographical particularism as well as from historic doctrinal and intellectual developments. But keeping in mind that North India is our main focus, the responses of Hinduism, which are obviously of primary importance, can, without too much violence being done to historic realities, be fitted into two main categories.[8] The first of these responses can be included under the blanket term of "Neo-Hinduism," which covers numerous attempts made in the last century and a half to relate Hindu religion and culture to the pressures historically associated with the establishment of British political power. It has sought to purge Hinduism of what had come to be regarded as corrupt elements, by declaring, on the one hand, that they were not integral to its structures and by asserting, on the other, that all religions have a common core of truth. Many of the leaders famous in modern India's social and political life would fall into this category, including Ram Mohan Roy, Vivekananda, Aurobindo, and, above all, Gandhi. In this response, which denies the importance of those outward characteristics that are usually regarded as definitive, Gandhi played a crucial role, not so much because of any particular theological subtlety in his teaching but because he made this interpretation of religion of central importance in Indian politics.

The secularism that is one of the most cherished goals of the dominant Indian political culture is not derived from modern Western political practice, as are so many aspects of modern Indian thought, but from Gandhi's translation of nationalist ideals into the vocabulary of Neo-Hinduism. The theological basis of Indian secularism is not a denial of the claims of religion but an assertion—one can say a profoundly dogmatic one—that all religions are true. Anything that appears to be socially harmful can be abandoned—what is left will be the kernel of truth. This is what Gandhi meant when he said, "For me, truth is God," which is very different in its implications from the Christian formula, "God is truth." For Gandhi and his followers such an interpretation of religion was the answer to India's most pressing political problem—the antagonism between Hindus and Muslims—as well as of such social problems as untouchability. Secularism, in the Indian sense, is an attempt to create the basic requisite of a nationalist state, a homogeneous population.

The Neo-Hindu, or Gandhian, solution will always have an attraction for men of good will, but patently it did not work. Many serious and knowledgeable students of modern India have wondered if Gandhi's use of a religious vocabulary—inevitably Hindu in origin—did not in fact exacerbate the political and social relations between the Hindus and Muslims. As A. B. Shah has suggested, Gandhi—and this is true for Neo-Hinduism in general—by overlooking the historically determined character of man's culture and institutions, misunderstood the intractable nature of India's social problems, especially the basis of conflict between religious groups.[9] Mistaking the form for the substance, Neo-Hinduism supposed that if it could be demonstrated that all religions had common aims, this would end conflict, not understanding that the modern religious labels were almost accidental to the deep divisions of Indian society. One might almost say that Gandhi, who was so deeply conscious of the need for personal purity, did not take seriously the problem of human passion.

There is another factor in the Neo-Hindu approach to conflict that must be noted: a seemingly complete inability to understand that Muslims and Christians, to the degree that they are committed to their faiths, find their identities in membership in a religiously defined community. For Hinduism at the deepest level, on the other hand, salvation is ultimately individualistic, concerned with transcending the social order. The statement that outside the church there is no salvation is both abhorrent and childish to a Neo-Hindu, while it must be fundamental to anyone who truly lives within the confines of the Semitic faiths. Neo-Hinduism's solution to the fact of religious pluralism is thus a denial of the basis of what to Muslims is the great reality—the sense of community. The grimmest commentary on the irrelevance of the Neo-Hindu answer is given in the story of the bitter religious riots of the last few years.

One turns, then, to the other category of responses made by Hinduism in coming to terms with the modern world: that of the groups known variously as Hindu communalists, Hindu reactionaries, or, as I prefer, the Hindu Radical Right. This response is represented institutionally by such groups as the Jana Sangh, the Hindu Mahasabha, and the R.S.S. They are, as I have suggested above, radical, not reactionary, because the goals they formulate and the solutions they propose would as truly transform Indian society as would those of the Radical Left. Their literature, especially in Hindi, is filled with programs for change, however absurd these may seem to those with different ideological commitments. The Hindu Radical Right does not appeal to the peasants, whose religious beliefs and practices have been scarcely touched by the modern world, but rather to those, particularly in the urban areas, who are most conscious of the pressures of change.[10] This means, one can hazard a guess, that the appeal of such groups will not decrease as modernization progresses in India—as liberals hopefully assume—but rather will increase.

The thrust of the Hindu Radical Right can be seen most significantly in attitudes towards the four major goals of the dominant political culture. These goals—national unity, social justice, democracy, and secularism—are not rejected by the Radical Right, but rather are transformed through redefinition. They allege that it is the dominant political groups who, through a false interpretation of the goals, are destroying India. National unity, they argue, means an integrated, homogeneous society; and this can only be found by recognizing that Indian culture and Hindu culture are synonymous terms. This means, of course, that the place of the religious minorities is at once called into question, for the essence of Islam and Christianity—the belief in salvation through membership in a collective social body—seems to be a denial of national unity. Territorial integrity, a basic concern for any modern nation state, is also given a religious coloring, for the threat to that integrity comes from such groups as the Christian tribesmen in the northeastern hills or from *India irredenta,* Pakistan. Social justice is also given a different definition—one, the Hindu Radical Right would insist, that draws upon the Hindu understanding of the nature of society, not upon the alien ideas of the West. There is vagueness in programmatic details, but with the continual references to the ideal of *dharma* as enshrined in the *varna* concept, it does not take a very imaginative reading between the lines to see who will be the hewers of wood and drawers of water. As for democracy, nothing in India, as elsewhere, is more easily shaped to special needs. A quotation from a Jana Sangh newspaper suggests the tone and temper of the democracy advocated by the Hindu Radical Right: "In any democratic country only the majority has rights. . . . Some Muslims will get terribly disturbed after reading this . . . [but] the minority will have only the rights which the majority bestows upon them at its pleasure."[11]

Secularism is, of course, the obvious area for redefinition, with the meaning given to it subsumed by the interpretation of the other goals of the society.[12] A succinct summary was given some years ago by M. S. Golwalkar, the best-known spokesman for the Hindu Right, when he stated, "The non-Hindu people in Hindustan must adopt the Hindu culture and religion, must learn to respect and hold in reverence Hindu religion, and must entertain no ideas but those of glorification of the Hindu race and culture . . . claiming no privileges . . . not even citizens' rights."[13] Such views are not put forward as part of any party's political platform, but they are part of the rhetoric of religious appeal. Such a quotation, however extreme and perhaps atypical, reinforces the point made at the beginning—that the Radical Right does not engage in frontal attacks on modernity so much as on other religious groups. The demand for a ban on cow-slaughter illustrates this quite neatly, for it is at once a way of embarrassing the government's devotion to secularism and of attacking Muslims.[14] A ban on cow-slaughter would be obviously sectarian legislation; but its symbolic appeal is very considerable, although it seems to be confined to the urban areas, having less impact on the countryside. The attack on Urdu in Bihar and Uttar Pradesh is defended as a movement towards national unity, but the goal is the homogeneous society characterized by the dominance of Hindu culture.

A rather bizarre illustration of the ambiguities of secularism was provided in 1969 when the Sankaracharya of Puri, one of the most prestigious figures of Hindu orthodoxy, began making public speeches in which he stated that ritual pollution and the idea of untouchability were scripturally sanctioned. Not surprisingly, he was able to quote chapter and verse.[15] The fierce public outcry that followed indicated how sensitive a nerve he had touched. The leaders of the Jana Sangh were content to say that they disagreed with the Acharya's interpretation of the shastras, but many spokesmen for the modernizing groups, true to the Neo-Hindu approach, began earnest exercises in textual criticism to show that the scriptures, far from sanctioning untouchability, preached equality and brotherhood. They had missed the point that the Acharya, who appears to be an intelligent man, was not seeking to obstruct change; quite the contrary, as his speeches made plain, he was wanting to bring about what he regarded as a change for the better, a society based on what he considered a rational view of human nature and the cosmic order.

The Radical Right defines itself not only in relation to Neo-Hinduism, but more importantly, in many ways, in relation to the Muslim community. The use of the word "community" is misleading in that it always carries with it a sense of cohesion and homogeneity, when, in fact, Islam in India is almost as fragmented as Hinduism. Muslim writers correctly insist that there is no Muslim response as such in India, since Muslim society is deeply divided by linguistic, cultural, social, and regional differences.[16] But as in the case of Hinduism, it is possible to identify two main responses to the pressures of modern social and political changes that are of great importance, with both being analogous to the two main categories of Hindu responses.

One is a movement of accommodation that has had rather different manifestations at different periods. In the late nineteenth century, as represented by Sir Sayyid Ahmad Khan and the Aligarh movement, it identified itself with a relatively cautious program of theological revisionism and a political platform that opposed the democratic implications of the Indian National Congress. Then, under the impetus of Gandhian nationalism in the 1920's and 1930's, a new variety of accommodation with both the modern world and Indian nationalism found expression in the group associated with Jamia Millia Islamia in Delhi. Irenic in its approach to other faiths and dedicated to a nationalism that could contain a religious pluralism, this group claimed for Islamic culture a significant role in the creation of a modern nation-state.[17] Yet, attractive as its approach is to outsiders, the reinterpretations of the Islamic role advocated by Jamia Millia Islamia do not seem to have engendered a very deep response from Indian Muslims. The reasons for this are partly theological, having roots in the nature of Islam as an intellectual system, but more immediately in the political and social conditions under which the Muslim community exists in India today.

Almost all observers would agree that whether the objective situation justifies it or not, a deep sense of frustration and anxiety characterizes much of the Indian Muslim community. According to Dr. Abid Husain of Jamia Millia University, it was the Muslims of India who had to pay the heaviest price for partition and independence, "not only in the form of spiritual and mental anguish but also in that of economic depression and educational and cultural backwardness."[18] It may be argued that the condition of Indian Muslims is no worse than that of millions of other Indians located in similar interstices of the social system, but the Muslims' perception of their situation as isolated from the mainstream of national life remains. There are two aspects of this perception, as a perceptive journalist pointed out in an article in the *New York Times* that was based on careful reporting. The Muslims are "a remnant in their own eyes," cut of from the Islamic state many of them in fact had supported; and because of this, they are in the eyes of the Hindu majority "a potential fifth column."[19]

Out of this situation comes the other response to social change, one that is analogous in many ways to that of the Hindu Radical Right. There are a number of Muslim groups that fall into this category, but the most important both in terms of its following and the articulation of its ideas is the Jama'at-i-Islami.[20] Founded in 1941 by Maulana Maududi to define and defend the concept of an Islamic state, it remained quiescent for some years after partition. Then, admidst the increasing frustration of the Indian Islamic community, it began to engender a wide response. Like the Hindu Radical Right, it accepts the general goals of the dominant political culture—national unity, social justice, democracy, and secularism—but then it redefines them. The Western idea of the state comes in for special denunciation as corrupt in its very essence, for the true state must be the expression of God's guidance. The idea of re-creating an Islamic state in modern India is, from a rational point of view, wholly fanciful; but the Jama'at-i-Islami represents the politics of a despair that is beyond reasonable political calculation. The rigorous simplicity of its teaching has a potent appeal for those who, as Principal Mujeeb of Jamia Millia has put it, "are ignorant of political procedure and the facts of political life."[21]

The Muslim politics of despair is not only the response to modern pressures within a modernizing society; it is also a response to the vision of the future sedulously propagated by the Hindu Radical Right. Muslims undoubtedly overreact to this propaganda, but its demands underline Muslim fears and frustrations. The political expressions of the Jama'at-i-Islami therefore become more absolute, more apocalyptic, more incapable of compromise with the secular arms of the dominant political culture. One is tempted to assume that in the Indian situation the Hindu Radical Right is alone responsible for the increasing violence and bloodshed of the communal riots during the last ten years, but there is reason for thinking that the Islamic extremists—the Muslim Radical Right, to maintain the analogy—have been responsible to some extent for bringing about the violence. The declaration by the Jama'at-i-Islami and other groups that salvation comes through communal solidarity and a return to obedience to God as the only sovereign ruler suggests to the more despairing that it is better to die in a righteous cause than to live in subservience to an alien culture. Death was the reward for such views. There were fifteen times as many riots in 1968 as there were in 1960. In 1967 alone, three hundred persons were killed, 90 percent of whom were Muslims.

While Hinduism and Islam inevitably claim the major share of attention in any discussion of the social role of religion in contemporary India, certain insights can be gained from at least a cursory glance at Christianity's place in what has been called the "uneasy mosaic" of Indian society. Although Christianity has had roots in India for a very long time, it has often been accused, because of confrontations between modern missionaries and such Hindu reformist groups as the Arya Samaj, with being an alien, foreign minority. Since 1947, Christians have been subjected to a considerable barrage of criticism and investigation, although at the level of the state, rather than the central, government. The general charge, however phrased, is the one already alluded to: that Christians owe primary allegiance to a religious community, and one, furthermore, that is extraterritorial in its organization. The specific outcome of this criticism has been the passing of laws in a number of states (such as Orissa and Madhya Pradesh) putting obstacles in the way of conversion. To most Hindus, and perhaps to many casual Western students, such restrictions may seem just. But as an acute observer of the Indian religious scene has pointed out, such restrictions are in fact the result of the tyranny of the majority.[22] They are also a denial of secularism, for presumably in a truly secular society, change of religious affiliation would not be a concern of the state. That so much is made of conversion in India is perhaps an indirect testimony to the point that the Hindu Radical Right and the Muslim Radical Right both make from their different perspectives: Indian society is fundamentally Hindu, and therefore conversion from Hinduism is an attack on national identity. "The dilemma of the Christians is the nation's predicament."[23]

I have tried to suggest that the vital social role of religion in modern India is not to be found in the numerous attempts at accommodation made by Neo-Hindus or Islamic modernists, but in the groups categorized as the Radical Right, both Hindu and Muslim, but especially in the Hindu ones. Their vitality is not demonstrated in an obscurantist defense of the past, but through an assertion of what they regard as a better vision of the future than that offered by the forces of social and political modernization. The very rapid and sweeping advances in industrialization will not lessen the conflicts and tensions but, rather, will exacerbate them. The actual areas of conflict have been the most modern of cities—Indore, Ahmedabad, and Jamshedpur—not the rural hinterlands. One can hazard the guess that out of the vitalities of Hinduism, and perhaps also of Islam, will come not lesser but greater confrontations as the lines are more clearly drawn in the future.

NOTES

1. One aspect of this theme is examined in Ainslie T. Embree, "Tradition and Modernization in India: Synthesis or Encapsulation," in *Science and the Human Condition in India and Pakistan*, ed. Ward Morehouse (New York, 1968).

2. Donald E. Smith, ed., *South Asian Politics and Religion* (Princeton, N.J., 1966), focuses on the political significance of religion.

3. An important exception is *Religion and Society*, The Bulletin of the Christian Institute for the Study of Religion and Society at Bangalore.

4. A. B. Shah, "Religion in Public Life," *Opinion*, Sept. 3, 1968, quoted in *Religion and Society*, 16.1:3 (1969).

5. M. N. Roy, *Fragments of a Prisoner's Diary* (Calcutta, 1950), Vol. I; and Rabindranath Tagore, "The Call of Truth," *Modern Review*, 30.4:29–33 (1921).

6. Gunnar Myrdal, *Asian Drama* (New York, 1968), I, 34.

7. Karl Marx, "The British Rule in India," in *K. Marx and F. Engels: The First Indian War of Independence, 1857–1859* (Moscow, 1959), p. 70.

8. For an interesting discussion of this point, see Richard Taylor, "Hindu Religious Values and Family Planning," *Religion and Society*, 16.1:6–22.

9. A. B. Shah, foreword to Hamid Dalwai, *Muslim Politics in India* (Bombay, 1968).

10. Craig Baxter, *The Jana Sangh* (Philadelphia, 1969), passim. Some of the most useful information on the attitudes and activities of the Radical Right comes from the publications of the Sampradayikta Virodhi Committee, an organization for opposing communalism, and from the publications of the Communist Party of India. The weekly *Organiser* provides insights into the thinking of the Hindu Right. It should be read in conjunction with its opposite number from the Muslim Radical Right, *Radiance*.

11. *Pratap*, Dec. 8, 1968, quoted in M. F. Farooqi, *Communist Party and the Problems of Muslim Minority* (n.p., 1969).

12. D. E. Smith, *India As a Secular State* (Princeton, N.J., 1963), and G. S. Sharma, *Secularism: Its Implications for Law and Life in India* (Bombay, 1966), examine the meaning of the secular state. One of the most interesting examinations of the philosophical implications of the whole question is Frank D. Van Alst, "The Secular State, Secularization and Secularism," *Quest*, No. 62 (July 1969), pp. 24–35.

13. M. S. Golwalkar, "We and Our Nationhood Defined," quoted in Farooqi, *Communist Party and the Problem of the Muslim Minority*, p. 8.

14. A. B. Shah, ed., *Cow Slaughter: Horns of a Dilemma* (Bombay, 1967), for an analysis of the anti-cow-slaughter movement.

15. Detailed accounts are to be found in the Indian newspapers for April 1969.

16. See Rasheeduddin Khan, "Uneasy Mosaic," *Citizen*, Vol. I, Nos. 6, 7, 8, and 9 (May 24–July 12, 1969).

17. For the significance of this movement, see Aziz Ahmad, *Islamic Modernism in India and Pakistan, 1857–1969* (London, 1967), pp. 254–57, and M. Mujeeb, *The Indian Muslims* (London, 1967).

18. Abid Husain, *The Destiny of Indian Muslims* (London, 1965), p. 129.

19. Joseph Lelyveld, *New York Times*, Oct. 28, 1968.

20. The pamphlet literature of the Jama'at-i-Islami Hind, New Delhi, both in English and Urdu, is considerable, and the materials of the Sampradayikta Virodhi Committee are useful for the Muslim Radical Right. See, especially, "Introducing the Jama'at-e-Islami Hind" (Delhi, 1966).

21. Mujeeb, *The Indian Muslims*, p. 403.

22. Frank Thakur Das, "The Dilemma of the Christians," *Citizen*, 1.10: 14–15 (July 26, 1969).

23. *Ibid.*

The Buddhist Model for Renewal: An Examination of Contemporary Buddhist Sangha in Asia

Minoru Kiyota
University of Wisconsin

Introduction

The Buddhist model for renewal presupposes the need for examining what Byron Earhart refers to as "the spiritual and transcendental dimensions of human experience,"[1] in counter-distinction to historical factors that shape religious thought. This is particularly so because Buddhism, like any other religion, is subject to the processes of "fossilization and renewal." Fossilization takes place when Buddhism fails to provide the transcendental insight to interpret historical realities. It is renewed when it provides this insight. The historical continuity of the Buddhist tradition depends on the constant cyclic feedback between the transcendental and the historical. The two are not unrelated. In Buddhist terms this feedback between the transcendental and the historical specifically refers to the feedback between the Buddha-Dharma and the Sangha.[2] The feedback formula will be applied to examine two specific subjects: the relationships between monks and the laity and between church and state.

This paper is divided into three sections: (1) the three jewels as a model for renewal; (2) the relationship between monks and the laity; and (3) the relationship between church and state. In passing, it might be pointed out that though Mahāyāna[3] presupposes universal enlightenment,[4] Theravāda, too, is capable of providing the "spiritual and transcendental dimensions of human experience." The theme that the Buddhist model for renewal is found in its own tradition, which this paper intends to call attention to, is articulated by critically examining both the Theravāda and Mahāyāna traditions.

The Three Jewels: The Buddhist Model for Renewal

The three jewels are the Buddha, the Dharma, and the Sangha. The Buddha is the object of faith; the Dharma is the object of understanding; the Sangha is the fellowship of men devoted to that faith and understanding, which are manifested through the practice of compassion (*karuṇā*). Faith and understanding transcend the bounds of established institutions. The Sangha is an ecclesiastical institution that relates itself to established social institutions through practice. In order to respond creatively to historical changes, Buddhism depends on the constant cyclic feedback between the Buddha-Dharma and the Sangha. This means that the Buddha-Dharma is the spiritual source of the Sangha. It also means that though the Buddha-Dharma transcends the bounds of established institutions, Buddhists must reassess the Buddha-Dharma with reference to historical changes, because the Buddha-Dharma has its meaning only with reference to the Sangha. Reassessment does not undermine the religious value of Buddhism; on the contrary, it is a means to prevent the fossilization of the Buddha-Dharma. The feedback between the Buddha-Dharma and the Sangha is the formula for Buddhists to contribute creatively to the development of their own culture and to articulate the religious value of Buddhism in contemporary society.

According to early texts,[5] the Buddha, in his first sermon at Deer Park, proclaimed, "I am the Tathāgata." Tathāgata is one of the many designations assigned to the Buddha, the enlightened one. Conze says: "Tathāgata can only be understood as tathā-gata *or* thathā-āgata, 'thus gone' or 'thus come,' 'thus' meaning traditionally 'as the previous Buddhas' have come or gone."[6] Yamaguchi analyzes Thathāgata into *"thathā-gata"* (one who has gone to the realm of nirvāṇa) *and "thathā-āgata"* (one who has returned to the realm of *saṃsāra*, that is, transmigration).[7] The term Tathāgata is frequently employed as a modifier for the three jewels.[8] The notion of Tathāgata, though not necessarily originating with Buddhists,[9] probably was an attempt on the part of the early Buddhists to identify the Buddha with a long tradition, but among the Mahāyāna followers there might have been a conscious attempt to identify that term with the notion of the union of *nirvāṇa* and *saṃsāra*, as Yamaguchi seems to imply.[10] In Tantric Buddhism, union is realized through *adhisthāna*, which refers to a function, practice, or action (sometimes a ritual) designed to bring about the merging of the Buddha's compassion with man's faith and understanding of the Buddha and Dharma. The Vajradhātu Maṇdala, also referred to as the Nine Assembly Maṇdala (one of the two basic forms of the Japanese Shingon Maṇdala), is a graphic representation of the interchange between *nirvāṇa* and *saṃsāra*. The path to *nirvāṇa* is the cultivation of wisdom *(prajñā)*; the path to *saṃsāra* is the cultivation of *karuṇā*.[11] In Mahāyāna, enlightenment consists of involvement in both *nirvāṇa* and *saṃsāra*. More specifically, the identity of *nirvāṇa* and *saṃsāra* presupposes that the vitality for involvement in *saṃsāra* is derived from *nirvāṇa*, while *nirvāṇa* maintains its validity only insofar as *saṃsāra* remains an issue of historical reality. Oldenberg therefore defines Tathāgata as "der Vollendete."[12]

The Bodhisattva[13]—literally, a universal savior—plays a prominent role in Mahāyāna literature, such as in the *Prajñā-Pāramitā*, *Vimalakirti-nirdesa*, *Saddharma-Puṇdarika*, *Sukhāvativyūha*, and other *sūtras*. A Mahāyāna Bodhisattva is a mortal who has renounced his own immediate enlightenment to carry on the role of a universal savior in the world of *saṃsāra*: he is the ideal mankind; he lives in the world of *saṃsāra* but derives the vitality for worldly involvement from the Buddha-Dharma. The *Saddharma-Puṇdarika Sūtra*[14] presents a lively scene, where the Buddha, who is about to go into extinction, calls forth the Buddhas, Bodhisattvas, and Arhats in order to delegate the mission of spreading the Lotus Dharma to those who qualify. He delegates that mission not to the "enlightened ones" but to those living in the "world beneath the earth," meaning, probably, the persecuted ones who live in the experience of human sufferings.

The Buddhist model for renewal is involvement in worldly, historical reality, and its vitality for this involvement is derived from the transcendental Buddha-Dharma, which may be identified as *nirvāṇa*, *tathā-gata*, or *prajñā*. The message of this model for renewal is the identity of *nirvāṇa* and *saṃsāra*, *tathā-gata* and *tathā-āgata*, *prajñā* and *karuṇā*. A Bodhisattva is a personality that is directed to the path of *tathā-āgata* and derives his vitality from *tathā-gata*.

Monks and the Laity

Sākyamuni first converted the five *srāmaṇa* (mendicants) in Sārnarth. He then preached in Rājagrha, Srāvasti, Vaisāli, and other places in the central Ganges valley, where he probably gained a significant number of converts. These early converts became, for the most part, monks, not laymen. The early Sangha was a fellowship of monks.[15] Sākyamuni's early disciples were men of good families *(grihapati)*, which implies that Sākyamuni recognized that the survival of the monastic Sangha depended on establishing a rapport with wealthy sponsors. The early Sangha was a community of monks isolated from the lay community, though laymen were urged to take part in the lay *uposatha*[16] (confession) meetings, which were generally held six times a month and presided over by monks. But by rule, monasteries were recognized as the precinct of monks. They were supported by the lay community, which presented offerings as a means to accumulate merit, a deeply rooted tradition in ancient India. The tradition that monasteries depended on the laity, without the loss of their rights as independent social entities, was probably possible in areas in which such a tradition already existed or in countries in which Indian influence had been dominant, such as Ceylon, Burma, Thailand, and Cambodia. The establishment of such monasteries in China and Japan, where Confucian ethics predominated and where alms-begging was not received sympathetically, required radical change.

The rule of morality distinguished the monks from the laity. Morality in Buddhism is referred to as *sila* or *vinaya.*[17] *Sila* originally referred to a quality, trend, or action brought about by a habit; it later became known as "wholesome action" or "good ethical conduct."[18] Buddhist literature frequently refers to *sila* as that which removes the impurities *(ḳlesa)* of body, speech, and mind and restrains "unwholesome conduct." *Sila* is, then, a personal restraint and the standard of personal conduct. Inasmuch as it is a personal matter, details of *sila* vary among monks, nuns, novices, and the laity, and even among schools and sects. But the basis of *sila* consists of five or, at most, ten items: abstention from (1) taking life, (2) taking what is not given, (3) sexual misconduct, (4) wrong speech, (5) fermented liquor, (6) eating after noon, (7) theatrical arts, (8) adorning the body, (9) sleeping on a high bed, and (10) taking money. Monks, novices, and nuns were required to observe all ten; the laity, the first five. The third—sexual misconduct—was rigidly enforced upon monks, novices, and nuns, but was relaxed to allow sexual relations between husband and wife. Inasmuch as *sila* is a personal restraint and is not imposed externally, a monk was expected to be his own judge and to suffer the agony of his own conscience if he transgressed any one of the items.

Vinaya originally meant instruction or discipline; it eventually came to mean the instruction designed to maintain the discipline of the Sangha (of monks).[19] Items taught by the Buddha to maintain the discipline of the Sangha were organized as the *Vinaya-piṭaka*, and eventually some two hundred, or even over three hundred, items were added on.[20] *Vinaya* therefore refers to a rule of conduct imposed upon an individual externally by the Sangha. It is restricted to disciplining monks, novices, and nuns, but not the laity. As a matter of fact, the laity was not allowed a knowledge of the *vinaya*. Gradually, the *vinaya* was expanded to include *sila*, and thereafter the distinction between *sila* and *vinaya* became obscure.

The fact that the *vinaya* constituted the rule of conduct for monks alone means that a clear functional distinction was made between monks and the laity with regard to enlightenment in primitive Buddhism. Nagao says that the *stūpa* at Sanchi symbolically illustrates the difference: the central mount, projecting the notions of simplicity, serenity, and stability, represents the ideal image of monks; the fence surrounding it, showing the bodies of women, children, wealth, *nāgas*, and *devas*, represents the ideal secular life.[21] The function of monks was to set a model for enlightenment; that of the laity was to support monks as a means to realize secular benefits and favorable rebirth.

It might be of some interest to point out here that the second Buddhist Council was allegedly held at Vaisāli, where commerce thrived. Since monks such as Vajjiputtaka, who favored the practice of accepting gold and silver and fermented liquor as offerings, were condemned, the council evidently favored orthodoxy. The Tibetan, Chinese, and Japanese Buddhists hardly seem to take the *vinaya* literally. If they did in the past, that tradition has not survived. The early Chinese Buddhist catalogue[22] tells that Kumārajiva (c. 350–409), a learned monk from Central Asia, was forced by the King of Kuccha into marriage to a princess. He came to Chang-an in about 401 and translated many Buddhist texts into Chinese. While in Chang-an, he did not live in a monastery but in a splendid mansion where he was surrounded by ten beautiful women offered to him by the Chinese emperor. Kumārajiva evidently was above cultivating the discipline for sexual abstention, and he undoubtedly directed his energy to more productive enterprises. The Japanese

Shinran (1172–1262) married, perhaps more than once. He produced the *Kyō-qyō-shin-sho*,[23] a Buddhist text that commands much respect in Japan. Transgression against orthodox *vinaya* is not a conviction of moral corruption, but adherence to the *vinaya* provides the possibility of fossilizing Buddhism. Transgression provides a new dimension for the reexamination of Buddhism and its renewal, as the studies of Kumārajiva, Shinran, and other prominent personalities in Buddhist history seem to indicate.

Ch'an Buddhism in China no longer depended on the offerings of the laity, and it established an economically independent monastic order. The "Commentary on the Sayings of Huai-hai" (720–814) says, "a day without work is a day without food."[24] Saichō (766-822) of Japan rebelled against the orthodox *vinaya* and established an independent platform of ordination and an educational curriculum, including such secular enterprises as road-building, shipbuilding, agriculture, well-digging, irrigation, and so forth,[25] at his Mount Hiei monastery, activities that monks and nuns in India were prohibited from being involved in.

These examples show that the Buddhist model for renewal in China and Japan favored lay orientation over orthodox monasticism, an orientation that involved a radical reinterpretation of the orthodox *vinaya*. This does not say that Kumārajiva, Huai-hai, Saichō, and others succeeded in establishing a lay Sangha; however, they did provide the moral strength to challenge orthodoxy, particularly the *vinaya*, and laid the groundwork for the development of a lay-oriented Sangha. Lay orientation is the crucial issue that Buddhism now confronts.

Maeda reports the inability of the Ceylonese Buddhists to involve themselves in active economic enterprises, such as fishing, primarily because of their insistence on adhering to the orthodox *vinaya*.[26] (The same can be said of the Cambodians, who are favored with Tonle Sap, one of the world's greatest fresh-water fishing grounds. The Tamils in Ceylon and the Vietnamese and Chinese in Cambodia form the source of manpower for the lucrative fishing industry.) Because of their monastic orientation, the Ceylonese Sangha is an exclusive body: "Rights to the headship of a temple, the inheritance of temple property, and kinship ties combine to make the ordination lineage the major institution of the Buddhist order of monks in Central Ceylon," according to Hans-Dieter Evers.[27] He continues, "If no property rights or only insignificant ones are involved, either the monks cannot attract any pupils at all, in which case the lineage will not be continued, or they may ordain pupils who are not related to them."[28] Wriggins says that a new caste system based on the degree of English comprehension is in the process of formation in Ceylon.[29] In this respect Christian-sponsored schools are favored insofar as secular education designed for developing a "New Nation" is concerned, according to Ikeda.[30] Badgley states that secular British colonial rule, rather than the traditional monarchical rule based on a Buddhist cosmology, contributed in bringing about administrative unity in Burma.[31] *The Annual Reports of the Department of Religious Affairs*, Thailand, contain interesting data. In 1926, there were about 210,000 monks; the figure for 1959 was 250,000. Though there was an increase of 40,000 in thirty-three years, the population of Thailand more than doubled during that period. The 1964 figure, inclusive of monks, nuns, and novices, was 240,517. Even disregarding allowance for population growth, the number of professional members of the Sangha shows a definite decrease between 1959 and 1964. The Thais may be devout Buddhists, but very few of them are willing to commit themselves as monks. Japan's new religions are quite successful inasmuch as lay orientation is concerned, but what they propose is nothing short of a restatement of a feudalistic ethics.[32] The Buddhist Sangha in Korea and Taiwan is split between the home-departed (celibate) monks and the home-based (noncelibate) monks. Noncelibate monks are institutional products of the period of Japanese colonial rule in these two countries. Ironically, noncelibate monks, though they may be less inclined to observe traditional discipline, are generally better learned in Buddhological issues, primarily because they are less resistant than the celibate monks to expose themselves to the products of contemporary Japanese Buddhist studies. Whether they will be able to actively promote Buddhism in their respective countries is beside the point, however.

Lay orientation is a decisive factor that contributes to the process of the democratization of the Sangha, but even in the basically lay-oriented Sangha of Japan, Buddhists have not yet formulated creative and concrete means to relate traditional religious values to the solution of contemporary issues. Functional division between monks and the laity is maintained in the Sangha of other countries.

Church and State

Legend has it that at the time of the birth of Siddhārta, a holy man descended from the Himalayas to prophesy that this child had one of two choices that would shape his destiny: to become a king and rule over the kingdom of the Sākyas or to become a Buddha and enlighten the people of the world. An ideal king, in the Indian tradition, is the *cakra-pravartana-rāja*, the king of the chariot wheel with which enemies are crushed. Buddha means one who exercises infinite wisdom and compassion. Siddhārta could not choose to become both. His choice to become *á sramaṇa* and eventually the Buddha meant that he had to renounce all forms of worldly desire. The Buddha followed this line of thought throughout his life and paid the price of his choice: he passively witnessed the conquering of Kapilavastu by the Kosalans and the massacre of the members of the Sākya clan. Ironically, the Buddhist councils—from the first one allegedly held at Rājagriha following the death of the Buddha to the one allegedly held in Kashmir in the second century A.D.—were traditionally sponsored by kings. This tradition was observed even as late as the nineteenth century.[33] It identified a king as the "Head of the Church and the Defender of the Faith."

Furthermore, Buddhism in Southeast Asia absorbed native folk deities—the *nats* of Burma, the *phi* of Thailand, the *neak-ta* of Cambodia—as well as *devas*, *nāgas*, the *linga*, and other Indian deities and cult practices. Folk deities are fertility deities, earth deities, and ancestral spirits, all wrapped up in one. They provide identity among the members of what Emile Durkeim referred to as "segmentary society," a self-sufficient, rice-farming, village community. The natives, who practiced fertility cults, were receptive to the Buddhist doctrine of *karma*—physical transmigration and reincarnation. Religious syncretism and belief in *karma* provided the psychological ground for the coexistence of church and temporal authority: Buddhism embraced local folk deities; kings embraced Buddhism, identified themselves as Buddha-rājas, and exercised control over all deities and people who worshiped them.

The principle of coexistence between church and temporal authority resulted in the assumption of church power by secular authority. Buddhism in Southeast Asia influenced the temporal power by supporting temporal authority, and temporal authority employed Buddhism as an instrument to unify the people: Buddhism permeated the masses by coalescing with folk religion; it gained the support of the state by subordinating itself to the state; and it prevented itself from becoming the apparatus for critical thinking among its devotees by involving itself in both enterprises. It molded itself into a system of doctrine to be accepted without questioning; it glorified the nation, sanctified the ruler, and promoted conservative loyalty. Kitagawa says, "More often than not, Buddhism accepted uncritically its assigned role, upholding the *status quo*, even serving as a spiritual tranquilizer for the oppressed by promising happiness in the world to come."[34]

Modern Thai Buddhism offers a good example of church subordination to state power. The June 1932 coup d'état led by a group of young military officers and civilian officials, most of whom were trained in France, overthrew the Thai monarchy and, in its place, established a constitutional monarchy. Buddhism was employed as the instrument to foster Thai tradition and pride: the tricolor Thai national flag represents the Thai race, the monarchy, and Buddhism. Monks willingly adapted themselves to the new political climate, a matter clearly demonstrated when some two thousand monks petitioned Premier Phrayao Phahon in February 1935 to place the Thai Sangha under state control in order to bring it in line with the democratic regime. The Buddhist Order Act of 1941 reorganized the Thai Sangha: under the Supreme Patriarch, appointed by the king for life, were the Assembly, the Cabinet, and the Court—the Sangha's legislative, executive, and judiciary bodies. The Assembly was composed of forty-five members appointed for life by the Supreme Patriarch. The executive branch consisted of the central administration, comprising four departments, and the local administration, comprising regional, provincial, county, village, and individual *wat* (temple) units, one administering the other in hierarchical order. The judiciary consisted of three courts, each with its head and ministers appointed from among the members of the Assembly by the Supreme Patriarch. Though the Sangha managed to function in orderly fashion for over a decade, sectarian disputes eventually developed. The Mahayut, the major sect, controlled over 90 percent of the country's temples and monasteries; but the Thammayut, the minor sect, managed to control half of the seats in the executive cabinet, probably due to its close relationship with the royal family. (The founder of the Thammayut was a member of the royalty.)

Marshal Sarit led a coup in September 1957. He had no patience with democratic processes; he felt that democratic processes would be ineffective for achieving national development. Sarit gained control of all facets of government and carried out drastic policies aimed at attaining his goals. He intervened in ecclesiastical matters. The Buddhist Order Act of 1962 centralized ecclesiastical power under the Supreme Patriarch. A note attached to the Acts on the Administration of the Buddhist Order says:

> The reason for enactment of this Act is that the administration of the Buddhist Church is not a matter to be based upon the principle of separation of powers for the sake of balance among them as is the case under the current law. Such a system is an obstacle to effective administration. It is therefore appropriate to amend the existing law so that the Supreme Patriarch, head of the ecclesiastical community, can command the order through the Council of Elders in accordance with both the civil law and the Buddhist disciplines, thereby, promoting the progress and prosperity of Buddhism.[35]

Sarit believed that national unity was necessary for national development. He appealed to Thai traditional values—monarchy and Buddhism—to realize it. The Sangha was reorganized to help foster national unity. A highly centralized administrative order of the Sangha, subordinated to the central government, was established: The Supreme Patriarch, appointed by the king, was empowered to issue commands; the assembly was abolished; below the Supreme Patriarch was the Council of Elders, consisting of some four to ten members appointed by the Supreme Patriarch, who in turn was the Council's president ex officio, while the Director General of the Department of Religious Affairs of the Ministry of Education became the Council's Secretary General ex officio; and administrative hierarchy, from the regional to the individual *wat* level, was brought under the control of the Council. The Council was empowered to disrobe any monk whom it considered undesirable. The present Thai Sangha is hierarchical, is modeled upon the Thai government bureaucracy, and is placed under it. The principle of the separation of church and state in the Thai context means that monks are deprived of their political rights, among them the right to criticize government policy.

The predominantly Mahāyāna Vietnam Sangha offers a direct contrast to the Thai Sangha, though belief in karma and religious syncretism pervade Vietnamese Buddhism as well.[36] The Vietnamese have an illustrious history of public dissent and revolt, perhaps because their country was under Chinese occupation for centuries. But during that occupation, the Vietnamese had mastered the Chinese art of bureaucracy; had domesticated the Chinese literary tradition, Confucianism, Taoism, and Buddhism; and had developed a social organization and a culture which were in no way inferior to those of the French, who entered Vietnam in the 1860's. Though Vietnam had produced no Buddha-rājas, Vietnamese emperors frequently employed monks as court advisors, such as Ngo Chan Luu, who served Emperor Dinh Bo Lanh (968–980); Van Hanh Thuyen-su, who tutored Emperor Ly Thai To (1010–1028) and whose name is now employed to designate the Buddhist University in Saigon, established in 1964; and Thuyen Lao To-su, the spiritual master of Emperor Ly Thai Ton (1028–1054). The Tran Dynasty (1225–1400) was the most glorious period of Buddhism in Vietnamese history. Based on this strong Buddhist tradition, Vietnamese monks challenged the status quo in the 1960's, though it must be added that the modern Buddhist revival in Vietnam can be traced back to the early twentieth century.

The problem of individual dissent against state power is an old one. Socrates defended his conviction about the supremacy of the individual conscience and the value of free discussion in the court of Athens, and he abided by the decision of that court. The alternative to death was exile, if he were to uphold his conviction; but exile would have disqualified him from being a socially and politically committed citizen. The dilemma that Socrates faced has yet to be resolved. The issue of individual dissent against state power was dramatically demonstrated by the self-immolation of Vietnamese monks, which was an effective religious demonstration but not an effective political one. The note left by Thich Quang Duc, the first monk to burn himself to death in the crisis of the 1960's, said: "I vow to sacrifice myself on the altar of the Buddha and by its merits to realize the perpetuation of the Dharma, the peace of Vietnam and of the world, and the well being of mankind. Homage to Amitābha."[37]

The glorious moments of Buddhism in Japanese history

were the Nara (710–781), Heian (781–1180), and Kamakura (1180–1331) periods. Buddhism permeated the masses during the one-hundred-year war following the Ōnin Rebellion (1467–1477), during which time the combined forces of the samurai and the peasants overthrew the aristocratically oriented political, economic, social, and religious structure. However, Buddhism succumbed to the powers of medieval *daimyōs* (military lords) in the late sixteenth century. It passed through the period of Meiji nationalism (1868–1912) without eliminating the feudalistic elements of the Sangha, such as the *danka* system established during the Tokugawa period (1600–1868). The *danka* is a legal ecclesiastical unit of families committed to a given temple, in which funerals and religious services are held, the deceased are buried, and annual festivals are observed and which, in return, requires its members to assume financial responsibilities for the maintenance of that temple. The Tokugawas conceived of the *danka* not only as a parish system but also as an administrative unit under its bureaucracy for keeping control of its feudal subjects. All subjects under Tokugawa Japan were assigned to a *danka* temple. A monk in charge of a *danka* temple possessed the right to issue certificates of identification (birth, marriage, death, family composition, place of residence, occupation, travel permit, and so forth), and he frequently usurped his position as an overseer of the citizens to act as a watchdog for the Tokugawas. The present *danka* temples, though they no longer represent an institution of watchdogs, nevertheless maintain the feudalistic mood and outlook of the Tokugawa period. For example, even today a Japanese seldom selects a faith of his own choice; he is committed by virtue of his family's tradition to a *danka* temple. As such, a *danka* temple today is merely an instrument for transmitting the religious tradition developed under the feudalistic mood of the Tokugawas. Its major activity is funeral services.[38] Furthermore, the facts that organized Buddhism in Japan allied itself with conservative elements in suppressing the labor movement, the peace movement, and parliamentary practices in the 1920's and supported aggressive war in the 1930's and the 1940's cannot be overlooked.[39] The defeat of Japan in 1945 produced confusion among the Buddhists, for the very idea that organized Buddhism had endorsed as a means to enable Japan to rise as a world power was discredited.

The rise of the new religions, particularly after World War II, poses a challenge to established Buddhism. The new religions of Japan are unique because they identify with the masses. However, the new religions cannot (and do not desire to) deal deathblows to the established religions, just as Kamakura Buddhism could not eliminate Nara-Heian Buddhism. The new religions will affect the established religions to such a degree that further simplification of the established doctrine and practice will be necessary to satisfy the common needs. How the new religions or the established religions will fare in the future will depend largely on their ability to relate traditional religious values to contemporary issues and to provide insight into the relation of the individual to his cultural and religious heritage in the face of intense industrialization and urbanization.

Conclusion

The Thai Sangha represents a case of church subordination to state power. It requires a critical examination of the vinaya and the church-state relationship. The Vietnamese Sangha (particularly the militant An Quang faction led by Thich Tri Quang) represents a case of the church challenging state power. In both the Thai and Vietnamese Sanghas, Buddhism is identified with nationalism; in both, *vinaya* is taken seriously. In Japan, *vinaya* has not been a serious issue since the twelfth century, generally speaking. Monks generally abrogated it. Nor is the matter of church-state relationship a serious issue today, as it was prior to 1945. The problem for Buddhism in Japan today is to identify itself with the masses and to contribute creatively to the solution of human alienation and anxiety. It must explain the meaning of human existence in an industrialized urban society, and it must point out the destiny of the Japanese with respect to their nation and to the rest of the world as Japan assumes an increasingly important role in international affairs and as Japanese ideological interest gradually turns outside their small island empire.

However, Buddhism, whether Theravāda or Mahāyāna, relates itself to existing socio-political institutions from a soteriological point of view. It has not yet developed a social and political philosophy. Specific requirements for the Buddhist renewal in Asia today therefore include a serious consideration for a creative and concrete proposal to solve the problems of human suffering *(duhkha)* based on the awareness that in its own tradition Buddhism offers a model for renewal, which is contingent on examining the "spiritual and transcendental dimensions of human experience" as the basis of religious change. The feedback between the Buddha-Dharma and the Sangha, the model for renewal, provides for the diversity of expression in individual countries, each expression representing a means *(upāya)* to realize the essence of the Buddha-Dharma. In Buddhism, the means is as important as the essence. The means is compassion; the essence is wisdom. Compassion is the means through which wisdom is manifested. The *Mahāvairocana Sūtra* goes as far as to say that "means is the ultimate."[40] The means in the *Sukāvativyūha-upadesa* is defined as the "transferring of merits one has accumulated for the benefit of others."[41]

The Tathāgata is the rational basis of Buddhist humanism; the Bodhisattva is the ideal Buddhist personality. The feedback formula requires a perceptive insight into what these two terms mean in contemporary society. The three jewels then become meaningful to modern Asian Buddhists, because the foremost concern of Buddhist Asia is not so much in molding itself to patterns of Western civilization but in preserving its own cultural and religious heritage and thereby contributing creatively and positively to world civilization.

NOTES

1. Byron Earhart, "The Interpretation of the 'New Religions' of Japan as Historical Phenomena," *Journal of the American Academy of Religion,* 37.3:248 (Sept. 1969).

2. Sangha is a Buddhist ecclesiastical order. Buddha-Dharma means the content of enlightenment.

3. The sixth century B.C. in India was the period of the development of agriculture and of the rise of the merchant class, monarchy, and criticism of the Vedic authority in the central Ganges valley. Within this social, economic, and cultural background emerged Śākyamuni. The generally accepted periodization of the history of Indian Buddhism is as follows: Primitive (the period when the Dharma as thought by Śākyamuni and his immediate disciples was observed and practiced), Abhidharma (the period of the commentators and sectarian schism), Mahāyāna, and Tantric Buddhism. Primitive Buddhism, which emphasized adherence to the rule of morality *(śīla)* as a condition to the practice leading to liberation *(vimokṣa)*, evolved into sophisticated Abhidharma academism; Abhidharma masters produced the *Abhidharma-mahā-vibhāsā, Abhidharma-kośa, Abhidharma-hrdaya,* and other *śāstras* (commentaries) and contributed to the development of the Adhidharma elite; Mahāyāna rebels challenged the Abhidharma elite, emphasized universal enlightenment, and composed the *Vimalakīrti-nirdeśa, Lotus (Saddharma-pundarīka), Sukhāva-*

tivyūha, and other *sūtras.* The Abhidharma tradition, in the form of Theravāda, is dominant in present-day Burma, Thailand, Laos, and Cambodia; Chinese Mahāyāna exercises a dominant influence in present-day China, Korea, Japan, and Vietnam.

4. The Sino-Japanese Buddhist tradition (as well as those of the Koreans and the Vietnamese) holds that *kalpa* (eons of time) *śīla* (the rule of morality), and stages of practices are not necessary requirements for enlightenment. It advances, in turn, theories of abrupt or instant enlightenment. Enlightenment in this traditional context is not necessarily a process requiring time and (ascetic) practices but constitutes the simple awareness of the inherent state of enlightenment *(bodhicitta).* The Chinese Hua-yen and T'ien-t'ai schools speak of abrupt enlightenment, theoretically; actually, however, they adhere to the traditional stages of *bodhisattva* practices, which number some fifty-two or fifty-three. It is in Zen and Shingon that abrupt and instant enlightenment is stressed most emphatically. Abrupt versus gradual enlightenment is a subject that has been argued for centuries among the Buddhists in Asia. Enlightenment is conceived of as abrupt from the standpoint of enlightenment per se, i.e., from one who has realized *bodhicitta.* Awareness of *bodhicitta,* however, may be gradual. The logic of abrupt enlightenment flows from the "whole" to the "part"; that of the gradual, from the "part" to the "whole." Thus, Zen claims that "the mortal mind, just as it is, is that of the Buddha." Shingon goes a step further and claims that "the mortal body, just as it is, is that of the Buddha." T'ien-t'ai claims that the ten worlds—of hell, hungry ghosts, beasts, fighting spirits, heaven, man, *sravaka* (Buddha's immediate disciples), *pratyeka-buddha* (self-enlightened ones), *bodhisattva,* and Buddha—are coinvolved and are of the mind. Hua-yen conceives of the world in terms of the law of coexistence and mutual identity of various elements of existence.

5. *Majjhima-nikāya,* I, 171 f.; *Suttanipāta,* 1114; *Theragāthā,* 1205, etc.

6. Edward Conze, *Buddhist Thought in India* (London, 1962), p. 172*n.*

7. Susumu Yamaguchi, Enichi Ōchō, Toshio Andō, and Issai Funahashi, *Bukkyōgaku josetsu* (Introduction to Buddhism; Kyoto, 1961), pp. 154–55. The italics are mine.

8. "Tathāgatam . . . Buddham namassāma; Tathāgatam . . . Dhammam namassāma; Tathāgatam . . . Sangham namassāma" (*Samyutta-nikāya,* pp. 236, 237, 238).

9. The line "dvijam drstvā tathāgatam" (having seen a person who is twice born) is found in the Mahābhārata. Cf. *Mahābhāratam, with the Commentary of Nilakantha* (Poona, 1929), XII, 146, l. 26. The Jains employ the term "tathāgaya," Cf. *Sūyagadamga,* I, 13, l. 2.

10. Yamaguchi, *Bukkyōgaku josetsu.*

11. Minoru Kiyota, "Shingon Mikkyō Mandala," *History of Religions,* 8.1:39–49 (Aug. 1968).

12. H. von Oldenberg, *Buddha: Sein Leben, seine Lehre, seine Gemeinde* (Berlin, 1881), p. 312.

13. The term *Bodhisattva* employed in the *Jātaka* refers to the title of the Buddha prior to his enlightenment. The term takes on a different meaning in Mahāyāna literature. For its Mahāyāna meaning, cf. Edward Conze, "Buddhist Saviors," reprinted from *The Savior God,* ed. S. G. F. Brandon (Manchester, England, 1963), pp. 67–82.

14. See the *Taishō Tripitaka* (hereafter abbreviated as *T.*), Vol. IX, bks. 262, 263, 264, chap. 10.

15. For details, cf. Sukumar Dutt, *Buddhist Monks and Monasteries of India: Their History and Contribution to Indian Culture* (New York, 1962), pp. 58–97.

16. *Uposatha* is the day of confession, or self-criticism. In primitive Buddhism, it was held two or four times monthly, depending on sites, usually on the days of the full and new moon (about the fifteenth and the thirtieth of each month, but sometimes on the fourteenth and the twenty-ninth as well). The lay *uposatha* was held six times monthly: on the eighth, fourteenth, fifteenth, twenty-third, twenty-ninth, and thirtieth.

17. Mochizuki gives a wide range of texts containing information on the rules of *śīla.* Cf. *Mochizuki bukkyō daijiten* (Mochizuki Buddhist encyclopedia), Vol. I (new ed.; Tokyo, 1954), pp. 902b–903c. See also Akira Hirakawa, *Ritsuzō no kenkyū* (Studies on the *Vinaya-pitaka*; Tokyo, 1960), pp. 278–88. For details on the *vinaya,* cf. *ibid.*, pp. 291–324. In English, cf. E. Frauwallner, *The Earliest Vinaya and the Beginnings of Buddhist Literature,* Serie Orientale Roma, Vol. VIII (Rome, 1956).

18. *Shih-sung lu, T.*, 23.1435:2a.

19. *Pi-na-yeh, T.*, 24.1464:852c.

20. Hirakawa, *Ritsuzō no kenkyū,* pp. 58–113, outlines sources for investigating the *Vinaya-pitaka.*

21. Gadjin Nagao, "Bukkyō kyōdan to bunka katsudō" (The Buddhist Sangha and its cultural activities), *Sekai no bunka,* Vol. III: *Indo-hen* (World culture, Vol. III: *India*), ed. Teruo Ueno (Tokyo, 1965), pp. 86–87.

22. "Ch'u san-tsang chi-chi," chap. 10; cf. *T.*, 55.2145. Also see "Kao-seng-chuang," *T.*, 50.2059:330 f.

23. *T.*, 83.2646:589–644.

24. "Pai-chang huai-hai sh'an-shih kung-lu." Cf. *Zokuzō-kyō,* Vol. II, bk. 24, p. 5.

25. *Kenkai-ron, T.*, 74.2376.

26. Egaku Maeda, "Seiron bukkyō gakujitsu chōsa chūkan hōkoku" (An interim report on the investigation of Ceylonese Buddhism), *Kanakura Festschrift* (Tokyo, 1966), pp. 360–61.

27. Hans-Dieter Evers, "Kinship and Property Rights in a Buddhist Monastery in Central Ceylon," *American Anthropologist,* 69.6:709 (Dec. 1967).

28. *Ibid.*

29. W. Howard Wriggins, *Ceylon: Dilemmas of a New Nation* (Princeton, N.J., 1960), pp. 202–3.

30. Chōsaburō Ikeda, "Mareisha to seiron in okeru etosu no hendō" (The changing character of ethos in Malaysia and Ceylon), *Ajiya kinda-ka no kenkyū* (Modernization of Asia; Tokyo, 1969), p. 384.

31. John H. Badgley, "The Theravada Policy of Burma," *Tōnan ajiya kenkyū* (Journal of Southeast Asian studies), 2.4:75 (Mar. 1965).

32. Minoru Kiyota, "Buddhism in Postwar Japan," *Monumenta Nipponica,* 24.1–2:136 (1969).

33. During the period 1868–1871, Mindon-min (1853–1878), the ninth Alaungphaya king, assembled eminent monks of Burma, who selected "authoritative" Buddhist texts and had their contents inscribed on the Kuthodaw, the now-renowned 729 stone *stūpas,* an event occasioned by the fear of British encroachment. The Burmese considered this occasion as the fifth Buddhist Council. The sixth, sponsored by U Nu, was held in Rangoon in 1954.

34. Joseph M. Kitagawa, "Buddhism and Asian Politics," *Asian Survey*, 2.5:4 (July 1962).

35. As quoted by Yoneo Ishii, in "Thailand: Church and State," *Asian Survey*, 8.10:869–70 (Oct. 1968).

36. Indian *dhyāna* was introduced to Vietnam by Vinitaruci in 580; Chinese Ch'an, by Vo-Ngon-Thong in 820. Pure Land (Sukhāvatī) took sectarian shape in China soon after T'an-luan (476–542) produced the *Sukhāvat ivyūha-upadeśa* Commentary, popularly known as *Lun-chu*. Pure Land became popular in Vietnam in the late sixth century. Ch'an merged with Pure Land, with the latter playing a more dominant role by the sixteenth century. Pure Land devotionalism paved the way for incorporating Taoist practices of incantation and magic, in direct contrast to the Japanese Pure Land tradition. The merging of Pure Land, Ch'an, and Taoism was complete by the eighteenth century.

37. The note was observed by and translated for this author at Vien Hoa Dao, Saigon, in July 1965. At that time, a small pot of cactus with white ashes sprinkled on its soil was enshrined at the side of the main altar. The ashes were the remains of Quang Duc and symbolized his spirit, which, the Vietnamese Buddhists claimed, is like a cactus: neither can be destroyed by fire. The pot serves as a constant reminder to the Buddhists of the mission that needs to be carried on—the preservation of the Dharma at all cost in the face of government persecution.

38. Cf. Taijo Tamamuro, *Sōshiki bukkyō* (Funeral Buddhism; Tokyo, 1964).

39. Munenori, Suzuki, "Bukkyō kyōdan no kiso kōzō" (Basic structure of Japanese Buddhist organization), *Nihon shūkyōshi kōza* (Essays on the history of Japanese religion), Vol. IV, ed. Saburō Ienaga, Iichi Oguchi, Mochiyuki Kawasaki, and Akio Saki (Tokyo, 1959), pp. 172–84; Taijō Tamamuro, "Nihon bukkyōshi gaisetsu" (Survey of the history of Japanese Buddhism), *Gendai bukkyō meicho zenshu* (Collection of modern Buddhist works), Vol. VIII, ed. Hajime Nakamura, Bun'yu Masutani, and Joseph M. Kitagawa (Tokyo, 1960), pp. 226–37; Kyuchi Yoshida, *Nihon kindai bukkyō shakaishi kenkyū* (Studies on the history of modern Japanese Buddhism; Tokyo, 1964), are the standard works on modern Japanese Buddhism composed from the historical and social perspective. Unfortunately, they do not cover the period after the 1920's. Saburo Iyenaga, "Nihon no kindaika to bukkyō" (Japan's modernization and Buddhism), *Kōza: Kindai bukkyō* (Modern Buddhism), Vol. II (Tokyo, 1961), pp. 7–35, is an interesting essay written with a Marxist slant.

40. *T.*, 18.848, p. 1a.

41. *T.*, 47.1963, p. 231b.

Lamaist Laity and Sangha in West Bengal, India

Beatrice D. Miller
University of Wisconsin

Buddhism came to Tibet more than a millenium after the Sermon in the Deer Park and centuries after Nagarjuna had expounded the "Doctrine of the Void." In its historical development in Tibet, Buddhism acquired certain distinctive characteristics. Sharing with other Mahayana traditions the great stress on the Bodhisattva career, it concentrated not on the role of the Arhat and the individual quest for Nirvana, but on the transmission and fulfillment of the doctrine whereby "all can become Buddha." Tibet's Bodhisattvas do not abandon their task after a few lives, but are believed to continue by incarnation through the generations. They manifest themselves as the *sprul sku*, known to the West as "reincarnations," or "Living Buddhas," and as the true Lama (bLa-ma).

Thus, despite the confusion and controversies that have arisen from too broad a use of the term "Lama," there is still justification for the use of the terms "Lamaism" for the Tibetan interpretations of Buddhism and "Lamaist" to designate those who adhere to these interpretations. Certainly, for the purposes of this paper, which will discuss the situation of these kinds of Buddhists in India, the general term "Lamaism" seems to offer far fewer possibilities for utter chaos than if it were to be sprinkled with "Tibetan-Tibetan Buddhists," "Sherpa-Tibetan Buddhists," and so on. Furthermore, such a designation should indicate that, although the scene is set within the present-day political boundaries of India, the Sangha and laity under examination do not represent a continuity of Indian Buddhist development since the early days of Buddhism in Bengal, nor the "return" to Buddhism sparked by Dr. B. R. Ambedkar in India in the 1950's. Rather, they constitute a relatively recent, that is, nineteenth century, "introduction" of Lamaism as a result of the political and economic developments in northern India in the past century and a half, during which India's borders expanded to include Lamaists within it.

To properly interpret the more recent relationships between Lamaist laity and their Sangha some reference to the relations that obtained between them in Tibet is in order. For more than three hundred years the Lamaist Sangha, or the monastic body, was an all-pervasive factor in Tibetan life. Prior to the developments of the last decades, the members of the Tibetan Sangha individually and corporately were the effective controlling elements in secular as well as ecclesiastical and doctrinal affairs. There is no need to recount here the broad scope of political, economic, and other authority vested in representatives of the monastic community. Suffice it to say that even in ordinarily secular fields such as commerce and trade, international relations, and domestic government, the Sangha's representatives held final authority. By contrast, no secular authorities could successfully hope to dominate Tibetan monastic matters, except for the periods of Manchu and Communist Chinese control. This overwhelmingly powerful secular and ecclesiastical authority is the classic picture of Lamaism and its lay-Sangha relationships that have become so familiar to both Western and Oriental scholars. It is a picture in which the multiple secular as well as religious roles of the Sangha have thoroughly colored and, to some extent, distorted the more familiar Buddhist ties between the laity and the monkhood.

For some purposes of analysis, however, we are fortunate in being able to examine Lamaist lay-Sangha relations in an area where the Sangha totally lacks these nonecclesiastical powers. I will focus this essay on the lay-Sangha relations obtaining in the Darjeeling municipality, Darjeeling District of West Bengal, with minor references to other parts of the district and adjoining areas and to some developments in Calcutta. Only for contrast or clarification will the classic picture be mentioned. The data on which this paper is based were obtained primarily before the upheaval in Tibet in 1959 and the mass influx of refugees into northern India.*

* The material is based on field investigations during the period 1953–1955, undertaken with a grant from the Ford Foundation, Board on Overseas Training and Research, in the Darjeeling District of West Bengal and Sikkim. It has been supplemented by subsequent research in the district supported by a grant from the National Science Foundation (GS-34), Washington, D.C., to the Department of Anthropology, University of Wisconsin, Madison, Wisconsin, 1963–1964.

The British annexed the Darjeeling District region west of the Tista River in the course of their dealings with the little kingdom of Sikkim. Annexation occurred in stages, from the 1830's to the 1860's. However, from the time that the British first began negotiating to acquire possession of the district, the nature of the population and its cultural orientations sharply contrasted with what had preceded British occupation. The former Sikkimese hinterland was radically transformed. Almost from the first, summer residences for government officials and for other European and Indian ruling families established Darjeeling as a highly Westernized community. Later the sparse Sikkimese population was further overwhelmed as the British brought in large numbers of Nepalese to clear the lands, to work the newly created tea and cinchona plantations, and, after 1857, to provide the British with a politically safe army.

To encourage these developments, the British reorganized the system of land ownership. All lands were government owned, to be rented out or given in permanent settlement for certain specific purposes that did not include the purpose of founding or supporting Lamaist monasteries or temples. Furthermore, the reorganization quite effectively deprived the existent monasteries of the landed estates that Sikkim had settled upon them. Otherwise, except for removing the Darjeeling monastery (now Bhutia Busti gompa) from the crest of Observatory Hill so that its activities would not disturb the Anglican congregation's Sunday services, British policy was primarily one of passive toleration. This meant minimal active interference with, and less support for, the Lamaist system. Thus, for the most part, the British were content to have Sikkim continue its supervision over most of the monasteries, despite a rising aversion of the Darjeeling laity to such an arrangement. Early in the twentieth century the British did go so far as to grant a Rs. 30 (about $10.00 then) monthly grant to the monastic school at Ghoom, the only dGe-lugs-pa (yellow, or orthodox, sect) monastery in the area. However, this act was designed for its effect on Anglo-Tibetan relations, not for its aid to the local Lamaists.

Despite the absence of active interference, the location of the monasteries and temples in the area of political India (thus, they were subject first to British and then to Indian governmental policy) guaranteed that they would lack the degree of independence and self-sufficiency that they enjoyed in Sikkim itself.

Thus, in no instance west of the Tista River did a monastery occupy the position of landlord or estate holder. Instead, the Lamaist adherents might find it necessary to acquire a suitable plot of land by leasing property from a Hindu or other landlord. Some donor or donors would have to assume the responsibility for meeting the terms of the lease, or the monastery could conceivably be seized. Furthermore, Lamaist monasteries and temples were not automatically exempted from taxation. Since Indian independence, there are only two grounds on which they can obtain tax-exempt status. Either the monastery or temple has to qualify as a public place of worship or it has to plead extreme hardship. The latter grounds further preclude the possibility of the monastery or temple holding any lands capable of producing support. The former grounds also encompass the monasteries and temples, such as that of Sakyong, and others east of the Tista. These monasteries were able to retain their landholdings because this territory was acquired from Bhutan at a later date, when British land policy had changed. However, the exemption from tax is applicable only to the actual monastery compound. In these instances the possible rental value of the buildings is assessed. The land occupied by the buildings is also assessed if it is classified as arable. There is also a proliferation of other taxes or cesses, for water, electricity, holding, conservancy, and so forth. All assessments are made on an annual basis. As long as the monastery remains "public," the assessments is waived in toto.

However, in order to qualify for such status, management of the "public place of worship" has to be vested in a group of trustees registered with the government as the "public's representatives." These trustees have to give the government an annual account of the monastery's financial and administrative affairs. As the representatives of the public, the trustees have to be selected by the lay adherents, not by the clergy. Clerical representation has to be minimal. The trustees have individual terms of office and serve for fixed periods. In other words, the financial and administrative affairs of each monastery or temple must be in the hands of a "lay managing committee" or else the monastery is legally viewed as a "private enterprise." As such it is subject to taxation and scrutiny as a source of private income. This safeguarding of the "public's" interest has been of major concern to the independent Indian government.

Furthermore, fulfilling the qualifications of a public institution produces not only the negative good of tax-exemption. It also offers the positive attraction of possible subsidies as schools or as "monuments to ancient tradition" or as "cultural heritages." Thus, today every monastery and most of the small temples in the district have their lay managing committees.

There are other areas in which British passivity and Indian activity have drastically altered Lamaist lay-Sangha relations. In both Tibet and Bhutan, and perhaps implicitly in Sikkim, the ranks of the Sangha were constantly replenished by the institution of the *lama ḳhral*. This was actually a form of labor tax, whereby one son from each taxable family (the definition of which varied from place to place) was drafted into the monastic order. Under the British, unless the monastery, such as the one in Sakyong, had claims on tenants who worked its land, it had no legal means to enforce the *ḳhral*. Under the Indians the concept itself is illegal, whether or not tenantry is involved.

Thus the monasteries in the district lack land, lack political power, and lack control, even over their own financial matters. To this inventory of "lacks" or diminutions from the "classic" situation must be added the effect of the institution's being the religious expression of a very small minority group in a secular or quasi-secular state. In Tibet and Bhutan, even in those instances where the monastery lacked wealth and political authority, it still offered great secular attractions as a channel for potential social mobility. In the Westernized urban milieu of Darjeeling the channels for education, for economic and social advancement, for political influence, and for status in general are far more extensive outside the realm of the Sangha. In fact, one's chances for social mobility are diminished rather than enhanced by the time spent within monastery walls.

Not only has the position of the monastic community been drastically circumscribed by the inhibiting regulations of a non-Lamaist government; it has also been altered by the peculiarities of the Lamaist laity in the area.

In Tibet, Bhutan, and Sikkim the monastery's lay community has been relatively homogeneous. The community has had a relatively stable historical and geographic continuity. The laity's ties with the local Sangha have also been relatively stable for a long period of time. The relations between the lay community and the Sangha had been shaped largely by political, economic, and social factors over which the individual members of the lay community had little control. In these "Lamaist

States" the monastic order had been either the source or the tool of the ruling group. As such it had been actively involved in welding individual communities into the broader cultural units. At the same time it had contributed to the jealous retention of regional or "national" distinctions, which frequently were associated with the predominance of a particular sect of Lamaism.

On the Indian side of the border all this is different. Here is a general Lamaist community, composed of representatives of many widely different groups. In effect, Darjeeling represents a cross-section of the total Lamaist population. There are the people from Sola and Khumbu in Nepal, who now are known collectively as Sherpa. According to tradition they had migrated from eastern Tibet, possibly during the sixteenth century. Since then they had been living under Hindu-Nepali control until they began to migrate as a trickle, then a stream, into the district. There are also Yorlmo, a people who trace their origins to the Ngari-Khorsum region of western Tibet. They had been under Hindu-Nepali influence for so long that they were being absorbed into the Nepali caste system. There are also the Amdowa from northeastern Tibet, the Khamba from the southeastern Khams region, and Ladakhis, as well as people from the central provinces of Tibet. There are Lepcha, originally a simple slash-and-burn horticultural people; Sikkimese, who are a mixed Tibetan and Lepcha group; and Dukpa, as the people of Bhutan are called. Not only is the Lamaist community heterogeneous with regard to ethnic background, but this heterogeneity is further enhanced by the fact that some members of each group probably had come to the District generations ago, while others came more recently and some are still coming. Thus the community is composed of grand old families that have lived in Darjeeling for generations and of individual "greenhorn" immigrants. With very few exceptions, almost entirely limited to the Yorlmo of Alubari and the Dukpa of Sakyong, they have not continued in their old pastoral or agricultural patterns of living. The vast majority left their herds, their fields, their families, and their homes behind—most of the anchors to their traditional ways of life. In their new environment they became coolies, porters, servants, laborers, shopkeepers, and entrepreneurs. In conformity with the basically European standards of Darjeeling, the men have cropped their hair and adopted Western dress.

In short, no matter when they came, or from where, they have been precipitated into a primarily urban situation and have become dependent upon a wage economy. Furthermore, the overwhelming majority of the population of the District is Nepalese. To exist in this milieu, all but the most recent arrivals have adopted Nepali as their *lingua franca.*

In their homelands the relations between the lay and monastic communities had been fixed at least as much by ancient political, economic, and social customs as by the laity's present or past religious sentiments. All these former props, however, could not continue in an area where the Sangha not only lacked the sponsorship or protection of the state, but was also stripped of its privileged position as landlord and as the gateway to the secular "better life." Therefore it comes as no surprise to discover that the majority of the present-day monastic population consists of individuals who have come to India as monks, having undergone their initiation and training in Sikkim, Tibet, or Bhutan. The proportion of monks who had served their novitiate in India as offspring of India-domiciled parents has never been large and is probably still declining. The only exceptions to this are to be found among the offspring of the noncelibate clergy, such as at the rNying-ma-pa Alubari and Sikkimese monasteries. In short, in most instances the district's lay community remains largely unrepresented in the ecclesiastical realm.

While the rigors of monastic discipline fail to attract an adequate supply of new members of the Sangha, the existence of the Sangha, as expressed in the monasteries and temples, is a necessity for the lay community. It, as the physical expression of the Buddhist triad, must provide the laity with the religious experiences that assure them of better "lives-to-come." The fact that the majority of the monks must be imported does not diminish the community's vital concern that the institution shall survive. The district laity's minimal role as a source of personnel for the Sangha is countered by the greatly expanded scope that the laity enjoys in managing monastic business. Most striking in this regard, of course, is the role of lay managing committees, already mentioned.

The lay managing committees help to unite the diverse lay communities into a general Lamaist laity. Since these committees must have dealings with the government and with the public, members of the committees are generally chosen on the basis of substance as well as of merit. To be a member of one such committee is itself an indication that the individual is recognized as possessing both these qualities. To be a member of several or all of these committees is evidence that one possesses those qualities in undeniable abundance. Thus, for example, in the 1950's Ging, Bhutia Busti, and Ghoom monasteries represented three different sects, namely, rNying-ma-pa, bKa-rgyud-pa and dGe-lugs-pa. They also represented different national ties, namely, Sikkimese and Tibetan. Yet many of the same names occurred in each monastery's lay managing committee. RNying-ma-pa Sikkimese, Sherpa, and Yorlmo sat on the board of the Tibet-affiliated dGe-lugs-pa monastery at Ghoom, along with bKa-rgyud-pa Sikkimese and dGe-lugs-pa Tibetans. DGe-lugs-pa Tibetans and rNying-ma-pa Sikkimese, Sherpa, and Yorlmo participated in the *combined* lay managing committee of the rNying-ma-pa monastery at Ging and the bKa-rgyud-pa monastery at Bhutia Busti. Exclusion of potential members from the committee was not based on community or on sect, but on personal factors such as animosity or distrust.

The power to select members and the extent of the authority of these lay committees varied considerably. It seems to have been correlated with the feelings of solidarity between the monks and the lay community. Officially, at Ghoom the selection of the lay managing committee members was supposed to be the prerogative of the monks. Clerical representatives participated actively in the committee meetings. On the other hand, in the case of Ging and Bhutia Busti, selection was a function of a lay "membership," and the clergy had no voice. In the latter situation the lay committee's functions extended even into areas that might normally be considered matters for clerical jurisdiction. The president of the lay committee had the authority to receive and to decide upon the applications of any new monks who sought to enroll at the monasteries. The committee apportioned the posts and duties that supplied sources of income for the holder. It appointed the head monk and other monastery officials and fixed the rates to be charged for all ceremonies. It could forbid the monks to seek extra contributions or to complain through any other channels. It even determined which monks were to handle the arrangements for observances, and it had enforced a written agreement from the head monk that he would abide by the committee's decisions.

Apparently in some instances these lay managing committees might even have had the authority to determine what sect affiliations were to be continued or instituted. Thus, the minutes of Bhutia Busti's lay managing committee reveal a raising of the question and a decision to continue the monastery's adherence to the bKa-rgyud-pa sect. In the case of a newly organized monastery in Calcutta in 1954, some lay members actively sought eventual dGe-lugs-pa affiliation, while others thought in terms of either Sikkimese rNying-ma-pa or bKa-rgyud-pa connections.

The lay managing committees had the functions which made them the effective governing body of the monastery. The whole area of "collecting and disbursing" had been removed completely from clerical jurisdiction and decision. The committee decided whom to approach for contributions and how to expend the funds that came into the monastery, even including the question of the salaries for the "stipendary monks." It also determined what the monks themselves were to contribute to the monastery's general fund when they officiated at particular monastic "concessions." The lay committee governed the disposition of properties bequeathed to the monastery or purchased on its behalf. An example of this authority is found in a general rule made by Ghoom Monastery's managing committee, which stipulates that certain buildings donated to the monastery should be used as quarters for "celibate monks only." It even decided which particular celibate monks were to receive permission to occupy this property.

In some instances members of the lay committee sat as *panchayat* to settle disputes that arose between various members of the clergy, even when these disputes may have had doctrinal bases. Thus, for example, in Ghoom's sister monastery at Kalimpong, disputes between Tibetan monks and monks raised in the district reached such a pitch a few years ago that open battle broke out between the two factions. Only the direct intercession of the Dalai Lama sufficed to produce an uneasy truce. In Ghoom this role was filled by the managing committee. The same factional disagreements and some of the same Tibetan personnel were involved. However, here, before the matter reached the same stage, the committee "convinced" the Tibetan elements to retire gracefully with a sizable contribution as a gesture of community regret at their departure. By contrast, in Tibet and in Sikkim there had been innumerable instances of lay disputes being referred to the monastic community for settlement. In other instances rival monasteries had even instigated such lay disputes. Monastic disputes had been brought before ecclesiastical hierarchs in most instances, or had been resolved by the ruler. Compare this with the district situation, where it has been the organized laity that has mediated, or instigated, monastic disputes.

Organized lay involvement with the affairs of the Sangha may take other forms as well. These other forms are more apt to pertain specifically to a particular monastery. Usually the involvement with the affairs of the monastery on the part of these organizations will be only a part of their total role, a reflection of the position of the monastery as a "community enterprise." In some cases, the formal organization is composed of all the people who comprise a particular community, so that there is little distinction between the ethnic group and the monastery's organized lay community. An example of this is found among the Yorlmo. The Yorlmo form one of the smallest Lamaist groups in the Darjeeling area. They consist of about two hundred families in Darjeeling and outlying groups in other areas of the district. They are one of the few Lamaist communities that have continued agricultural activities, although they, too, are caught up in the urban patterns of Darjeeling. About fifty years ago a well-to-do Yorlmo leased land from Alubari's landlord, the Maharaja of Burdwan. He donated the plot as a site for a Yorlmo monastery. The continuing upkeep of the monastery is a function—perhaps the main function—of an organization known as the Yorlmo Sogchi *(tshogs-gcig)*, or Committee of the Whole. Both monks and laity belong. The Yorlmo from the other areas are also members. Thus the monastery at Alubari is truly a "community project," with the entire community formally organized and empowered to take charge of the monastery's secular well-being.

A variation of this occurs in Calcutta, where a mixed community of Sikkimese, resident Tibetan, and Sherpa Lamaists constitute the Himalayan Buddhist Association, which initiated the drive for a monastery. Calcutta's Himalayan Buddhist Gompa, as it is called, is a community project basically similar to the Yorlmo Alubari Gompa, except that the community differs because of its composite nature. In Calcutta the component elements of the heterogeneous community were each too small and too poor to function separately. The Association and the monastery serve all elements in forming a distinct community within the milieu of Calcutta.

Sometimes these formal lay organizations are initiated for

a specific purpose and then disband after having met the particular crisis. In Sakyong, the Dukpa community at one time had been organized into an all-inclusive organization. This organization rescued the Sakyong monastery when it was in danger of having its lands auctioned off to pay for the debts incurred by a dissolute head monk. Eventually, after having designated a lay managing committee that was responsible for the monastery's secular management, the association dissolved. In each of these instances and in numerous others the organized lay community voluntarily has assumed the task of founding or supporting a local monastery.

These voluntary associations usually have other functions on behalf of their members. They also act as mutual-aid societies, community councils, disciplinary bodies, and more-or-less-official representatives of their membership vis-à-vis the rest of the population in the area. Their role in relation to the monastery reflects the fact that the Sangha is an integral symbol not only of their religion, but also of the community's identity.

Despite the variations to be found in the extent and nature of community support for the various monasteries, the relationship between the laity and the monastery gives the laity effective control and, in some cases, outright ownership of the monastery. Whether this control is expressed in the form of a membership organization—such as in the Yorlmo, Dukpa, and Calcutta examples—or as lay managing committees, the monasteries are expressly regarded as belonging to the community, rather than as the community belonging to them. This difference in attitude can be seen most clearly in the power vested in the lay managing committees, the community's or the "public's" representatives.

Certainly the foregoing presents sharp distinctions between the "classic" Tibetan pattern of community-monastery relations and those found on the Indian side of the border. In no secular sphere can the India-based monastery claim the community or its members as its clients or subordinates. Rather, the situation is reversed and the monastery itself is completely subordinate, in the secular realm, to the community upon which it must depend for support and protection. The Sangha looks to the lay community as mediator and protector, roles more usually assigned to the monastic order. Only in the ecclesiastical or spiritual realm does the lay community assume its familiar dependent or subordinate position.

Even here, however, the altered relationship in the secular sphere of activity leaves its mark on the local laity. For example, the diminishing supply of local novices means that the opportunities for religious training and indoctrination have been curtailed. For the bulk of the laity this is even more true. Parents take their children with them when they make offerings or participate in observances at the monastery. Growing up in a predominantly Nepali-speaking milieu, many of the children and young people cannot follow or understand much, if any, of the intoned chants. Barriers to communication are further imposed by the fact that at least some members of the clergy are relative newcomers to the area and cannot explain or expound in Nepali. Miscellaneous adults explain the significance of the rituals and the reasons for respecting the monks. Frequently, but not necessarily, these adults are members of the Sangha. However, in any event, they are acting less in their monkly capacities and more in the role of parental surrogates and informed elders.

There have been some very telling commentaries on this minimal indoctrination by the monasteries in the district. One informant confided that he instructed his children, before they went abroad for higher schooling, to read Waddell and Bell's books on Tibetan religion so that they would be adequately prepared to answer questions about their religion. The Calcutta Association once desired to import Bhutia Busti's *'cham* (masked dance ritual) for a "benefit" performance and had to be coldly informed that the *'cham* was a religious ceremony, not just a spectacle. The Calcutta performance would have had to take place at sometime other than the traditional date, because the monks were needed in Darjeeling during the proper period. The Calcutta suggestion was comparable to some newly established cathedral requesting the performance of a Christmas High Mass in July in order to raise funds. Yet the incongruity did not seem to have been recognized by the lay committee that had made the request.

With all the limitations and restrictions incurred by the Sangha's position in India, the question inevitably arises, is Lamaism in India moribund? Stripped of the multiple facets that made Lamaism dominant in Tibet, can Tibetan Buddhism compete against the much more powerful pressures and attractions of Hinduism and Christianity to which its own potential adherents are constantly subjected? For that matter, can Buddhism of any sect, dependent as it is upon the presence of a Sangha, survive in situations where there is a political authority that is indifferent, if not actively hostile, toward Buddhism? Does lay support of the Sangha require the impetus of active political approval? Or must one at least assume that the Sangha can only depend upon the support and alms of a *majority* population, because such support and such alms have been instilled by tradition and backed by mass consensus? Despite its apparent disabilities, the Lamaist Sangha-lay picture in the Darjeeling District provides some surprising answers to the above questions.

The laity that instructed their children to read Western evaluations and discussions of their own doctrines had themselves felt the full weight of British-supported Christian missionary attempts. Schooled in Catholic and Anglican parochial institutions, reading and hearing about the "demonolatry" and "depravity" of their particular schools of Buddhism, twitted by fellow Buddhists—with *metta*, of course—about the alleged corruption and venality and generally unworthy behavior of their monks, the laity has not only been actively supporting the monasteries that it had more or less inherited from the past, it has also been continually establishing new monasteries and temples.

In the reports of Catholic and other missionaries one can see glowing accounts of the numbers of Hindu-Nepalese who have been converted despite the barriers imposed by the caste concept of pollution. By contrast, converting a single Lamaist is compared, in their records, to attempting to climb Mt. Kanchenjunga. The only successful conversions had occurred among minor children who had been taken into the various missions because they had been "abandoned," or were adjudged to be by the missionaries, and among Lepcha villages that had fallen under foreign control during the first period of British expansion into the area, that is, before Lamaism had been solidly established among them. Even conversion in youth seems to be unreliable. One of Darjeeling's most active Lamaist lay supporters in the 1950's had shed his Christianity long before he lost his sobriquet of "Je-su" Pemba.

Groups that had begun to adopt some of the Hindu caste characteristics of their Nepalese rulers have been progressively "de-Hinduized" in the Darjeeling District. While Alubari monastery-lay communities have remained basically Yorlmo, some Yorlmo have begun to participate in the other lay managing committees. Sherpa who have lived in Darjeeling have returned to their Nepalese homeland, and some have successfully eliminated there the beginnings of caste ritual practices and pollution/purification concepts.

After the Tibetan Uprising of March 10, 1959, the situation of the monasteries in the Darjeeling District, like that of monasteries in Sikkim, Bhutan, and other parts of northern India, changed radically. Not only did His Holiness the Dalai Lama and much of the dGe-lugs-pa hierarchy come down into India; many major incarnates, hierarchs, and other highly learned and highly venerated monks of all the sects also found their way across the border. The district's laity, as well as the lay refugees who took up residence there, had the unprecedented experience of having in their midst the almost legendary "greats" of their faith. Old gompas such as Bhutia Busti experienced a renascence with the influx of newly acquired monks from Tibet. In fact, in the early 1960's the presence of the revered Karmapa Rimpoche, hierarch of the Ka-rma bKa-rgyud-pa Sect, currently established at Rumtek, Sikkim, transformed Bhutia Busti into a bustling teaching monastery, a role it had not known for generations, if ever before. The Lama Kalu Rimpoche, of the 'Brug-pa bKa-rgyud-pa school, while residing at previously somnolent Sonada, below Darjeeling, had attracted a sizable number of a new class of Sangha members—Western youths, some "hippies" and others presumably fully absorbed in the doctrine. Countless other Rimpoches and Geshes have taken up temporary or more-or-less-permanent residence in the district. Clusters of monks and lay devotees have joined them there. New gompas have sprung up to accommodate and honor some of these. In other instances temporary quarters, such as shops and houses, have been rented. The refugees have also provided young, newly ordained monks who assure the district of an enlarged Sangha for at least the immediate future.

The Theravadin claims to spiritual superiority and more accurate adherence to the teachings of the Buddha have made a considerable impression upon some Lamaists of the district. The reappearance of Burma and Ceylon as independent nations in which Buddhism was the dominant religion has led to several pan-Buddhist conferences which have been attended by both lay and monastic members of the Lamaist communities, who have returned from these conferences with *strengthened* Lamaist convictions. They have seen similarities in practice within Sinhalese Buddhism and Lamaism. Both had masked dances, both had local deities who needed propitiation, and both had some corrupt monks. However, as one lay Lamaist delegate phrased it, there was "an honest or open corruption to be found among the Lamaist monks," who did not need to conceal their interest in money and the things of this world. And, in terms of doctrine, Lamaism still "offers its hope, its aim, that eventually all can become Buddha."

Here, perhaps, lie the answers to the questions that were posed earlier. In the theme of the Bodhisattva career and the deliberate rejection of the "selfish" quest of the Arhat, the Lamaist communities find both reassurance and reaffirmation of their faith. Whether their Sangha grows or shrinks in number, whether accommodations must be made between the cloistered, celibate ideal and the realities of life in a modern, secular state, there will always be some who will be embodied Bodhisattvas. Despite the numbers of venal or mediocre monks, there will be some who are truly capable and who still selflessly continue through the cycles of rebirths to help and to lead the unenlightened.

Rissho Kosei-kai: A Cooperative Buddhist Sect

J. Stafford Weeks
Monmouth College
Monmouth, Illinois

Rissho Kosei-kai stands as one of several amazingly successful postwar religious movements in Japan. Since its founding in 1938 it has grown to a membership of about three million in a country of one hundred million; it possesses one of the largest and most striking places of worship in the world, the Great Sacred Hall (Daiseido) in Tokyo; and it is continuing to grow and is expanding its influence into the United States, where there are "branch churches" in Honolulu and Los Angeles. In the years immediately after World War II, Rissho Kosei-kai was the fastest growing of the "new religions,"[1] although it has since been overshadowed by the even more spectacular growth of Soka Gakkai.

The primary purpose of this essay is to document the cooperative spirit that has marked Rissho Kosei-kai and to note some factors that may have contributed to its approach. "Cooperation" is used here to refer to the fact that Rissho Kosei-kai is willing to work with individuals and organizations related to other religious traditions, and to do so without overt efforts to undermine or subvert the faiths of the others. In part this is due to the tolerance so characteristic of Buddhism, and in part it is due to factors in Rissho Kosei-kai's own history and situation. A secondary purpose will be to note some differences between Rissho Kosei-kai and Soka Gakkai with regard to cooperation with other religions. This contrast is significant because Rissho Kosei-kai and Soka Gakkai are similar in their use of the *Lotus Sutra* and the *Daimoku* and in their Nichiren-oriented heritage.

In the "Catechism of Rissho Kosei-kai" the final question and the answer to it show that the organization is committed to a policy of cooperation with other religions:

> Q: *It is said that Risshō Kōsei-kai is very positive about cooperation between different religions, but how is this cooperation being promoted?*
>
> A: At present President Niwano holds several important offices, such as chairman of directors of the Union of the New Religious Organizations in Japan, councillor of the Japanese League of Religions, executive director of the Religions Center, member of the Religious Juridical Persons Council of the Ministry of Education, etc.
>
> The Union of the New Religious Organizations in Japan is an association of new religious organizations founded during the last thirty or forty years. At present more than a hundred such organizations belong to it, only fifteen years after its birth. Though they differ in doctrine and ritual, they cooperate on good terms and are eager to exchange their experiences with each other.
>
> The Religions Center was established by leaders in the fields of business, education, religion, etc., in order to cultivate the religious mind in the Japanese and to make Japan a great nation through a nation-wide religious campaign under the slogan, "Faith to All men!"
>
> Besides feeling the urgent need to cooperate with Christianity for the realization of world peace, President Niwano attended the Second Vatican Council, as a special guest, and met Pope Paul VI.
>
> Thus, in this organization President Niwano, leading all members, pledges his efforts to realize the cooperation of religions not only in Japan but in the whole world.[2]

Evidence of the cooperativeness of Rissho Kosei-kai is found both in the official literature and in the record of what the organization does. President Niwano was one of the participants in a Peace Delegation of Religious Leaders in 1963, visiting, among others, Pope Paul VI, Dr. Visser t'Hooft, who was then General Secretary of the World Council of Churches, and Archbishop Ramsey of the Anglican Church. This visit brought him into contact with many religious leaders in the West, a further development of which was President Niwano's attendance at the opening sessions of the Second Vatican Council Meetings in 1965.[3] His description of the occasion deserves inclusion here:

> It was in the evening of the 15th when I saw Pope Paul VI. I greeted him by joining the palms of my hands according to the Buddhist custom. As the Pope extended his hand, I did so too. Then he held my hand with both his hands so that I strongly held his hands with both my hands too. During the interview we kept our hands together. This strong shaking of hands expressed the cooperation, friendship and mutual understanding between Buddhism and Catholicism in a very special way. The determination of going on as a go-between for the two great religions was deeply impressed in my mind on that day.
>
> During the talk with the Pope, I could not but feel that despite the difference between Buddhism and Catholicism, both are the same in their essence. . . .
>
> Although there are differences with regard to the words and teaching, it may safely be said that Catholicism is the same as Buddhism with regard to what is essential, that is, the way for mankind to attain peace and the way for human beings to live. Sakyamuni says, "All are the one Buddha vehicle, neither two nor three." I had never been more convinced of the truth of this word than during my audience with the Pope. . . .
>
> Now, "religious cooperation" is being promoted on a world-wide scale. Even Catholicism, which was said to be exclusive, is praying for the other religions.[4]

Their current publications indicate that the openness of Rissho Kosei-kai toward other religions is, if anything, being extended. This year the *Kosei Times*, a monthly English-language newspaper, is running a series of articles on "The Great Dialogue and the Way to World Peace." The "Great Dialogue" referred to is the conversation between different religions. So far in the series there have been articles by a Roman Catholic, an Anglican, a Methodist, a United Presbyterian, and a Unitarian-Universalist. The last-named group has had especially close relations with Rissho Kosei-kai. In Tokyo some of the staff people of Rissho Kosei-kai have joined in the Unitarian-Universalist Fellowship Discussions and have established a student exchange with that group in America. Recent issues of the *Kosei Times* have included references to the attendance of President Niwano and three of his staff persons at a meeting in

Turkey of the Interim Advisory Committee for a World Conference on Religion and Peace;[5] to an address by President Niwano on "Buddhists Dream of World Brotherhood," in which cooperation with other religions is praised;[6] to President Niwano's being elected Chief Director of the Japan Religions League and to his plan to attend a meeting in Boston of the International Association of Religious Freedom;[7] and to Rissho Kosei-kai's joining with other religious groups to protest the Yasukuni Shrine Bill.[8] President Niwano's address in the August 1969 issue of the *Kosei Times* carries on in the same vein. Buddhism is there characterized as "vast and boundless, tolerant and compassionate. It is not antagonistic toward Christianity, Islamism, Confucianism or any other existing true religion. . . . Some of their doctrines are identical with the Dharma, though in different expressions. There is but One Universal Truth. Its explanations are many."[9]

The cooperative spirit of Rissho Kosei-kai has not reduced the missionary zeal of the movement. One slogan derived from the Religions Center in Japan is "Faith to All Men." This phrase has an inherent ambiguity in it. It can mean that all men should come to have faith in Rissho Kosei-kai, or it can refer to "an age when mankind unites in the spirit of religious cooperation"[10] and lives in peace and happiness. The latter is the explicit and official meaning of "Faith to All Men." "This society, feeling its mission as a guiding and driving force in the movement of Faith to All Men on the basis of religious cooperation, endeavours to develop this movement from something merely national into a movement covering the whole world to prevent it from remaining empty words."[11] The mission *(michibiki)* of Rissho Kosei-kai is thus related to "Faith to All Men," yet its direct aim is to lead people to become members of this particular organization. An official publication calls for "a pioneer action to open the nation's eyes to the true faith. We, aiming at the perfection of character, should show by our deeds what a splendidly guided organization Risshō Kōsei-kai is. This is nothing but *michibiki*."[12] The mission thrust of the organization and its cooperation with other religions at times seem to be interrelated. It is almost as though the mission of the group is to further a world religion that includes all men of faith at the same time that the cooperative stance of the organization is seen as an asset in mission work because it improves the public image of the organization. For Rissho Kosei-kai a cooperative spirit has been effective in bringing in new members and in strengthening the organization. It "works."

The contrast between Rissho Kosei-kai and Soka Gakkai is never clearer than when their mission efforts are examined. Soka Gakkai's traditional *Shakubuku* (break and destroy) methods are very critical of other religions. This method is no longer promoted by the organization, but it still persists. While the officials who explain Soka Gakkai's purpose and work are respectful of the faith of others, many can testify that the attack on their faith by Soka Gakkai members was a most disturbing experience.[13] This approach has elicited much criticism of the sect, but it has been effective in bringing in many new members. Rissho Kosei-kai, on the other hand, has tended not to criticize other faiths.[14] Rather, it has stressed the things it has in common with other religions and has presented itself as a vital religion that brings happiness and well-being to the individual and peace to the world. For Rissho Kosei-kai, this approach has also worked well. Both of these groups gain from the enthusiasm that so often marks a new movement, but the ways in which they express their enthusiasm are quite different.

In view of the fact that Rissho Kosei-kai and Soka Gakkai are both related to Nichiren and use the *Lotus Sutra*, it is fitting to ask why Rissho Kosei-kai has such a cooperative spirit toward other religions. Nichiren himself is usually remembered for his violent opposition to Zen and Amida Buddhism.[15] Soka Gakkai reflects the same general attitude in its opposition to other religions, even to Shintoism, which is so deeply rooted in the Japanese psyche.[16] It will be argued in this paper that there are at least five elements that may contribute to the fact that Rissho Kosei-kai tends to cooperate with other religions: (1) Cooperative elements can be seen in the Nichiren–*Lotus Sutra* tradition; (2) some events in the early history of Rissho Kosei-kai have tended to relate it to other religions; (3) the warm and inclusive personality of President Niwano has tended to produce a spirit of cooperation in the movement; (4) some socio-psychological factors function at the present time to support the mood of openness toward other religions; and (5) many of the doctrines of the movement support the idea of cooperation with other religions.

1. In the first place it should be noted that the Nichiren–*Lotus Sutra* tradition provides some basis for a cooperativeness in Rissho Kosei-kai. Nichiren was a much more complex man

than he would seem to be in most of the angry portraits of him in textbooks. His life falls into two quite distinct periods. In the first he was seeking to call the nation to use the *Lotus Sutra,* to reform, to be the great Japan that he envisioned. This period, when he was exiled and narrowly escaped execution, makes fascinating reading; but his later period, which is largely overlooked, showed a more irenic spirit and involved an effort to create a center from which spiritual power could flow forth.[17] President Niwano, in a personal interview with this writer, argued that Soka Gakkai follows the early Nichiren, while Rissho Kosei-kai takes the later Nichiren as its model.[18]

It is also true that the two groups interpret Nichiren differently. Soka Gakkai makes Nichiren the true Buddha, replacing Sakyamuni.[19] Nichiren is thus the central figure for that movement. On the other hand, Nichiren is important for Rissho Kosei-kai because he recognized the value of and advocated the use of the *Lotus Sutra.*[20] It is my impression that Nichiren's importance is declining in Rissho Kosei-kai. The publications say relatively little about Nichiren and much about "Fundamental Buddhism," a uniting of the *Lotus Sutra* with the Four Noble Truths and other teachings of Sakyamuni.[21] Nichiren's mandala is being replaced with figures of the Eternal Buddha as the object of worship.[22] It is true that Nichiren's *Daimoku,* "Namu Myoho Renge kyo" (Adoration to the *Lotus Sutra*), is still used, but it honors the *sutra* rather than the author of the phrase.

The *Lotus Sutra* itself contains two passages that have opened the way for Rissho Kosei-kai's cooperation with other religions. It must be added that these passages do not require such a cooperative attitude, but they permit it. The *sutra* does not limit religious cooperation. These passages make possible both Rissho Kosei-kai's cooperative attitude and Soka Gakkai's hard line toward other religions. The two passages are extensively used by both of these groups. The first is chapter 2 of the *sutra,* where there is a discussion of *hoben,* which is variously translated as "tactfulness" or "expediency."[23] The point of it is that Buddha used all sorts of *means* to bring people to enlightenment. These means need not be absolutely and eternally true; they may even be untrue in a literal sense. The truth of them is not to be judged in terms of how well the statement conforms to reality; rather, the truth is what achieves the Buddha's objective.[24] This concept of *hoben* can be used either to abandon a former practice or relationship or to introduce a new one. Professor Kubota feels that Rissho Kosei-kai has consciously used *hoben*—the principle of expediency—to adjust its message to the needs of the people, thus instituting new patterns.[25] President Niwano justified the shift from the Nichiren mandala to the figure of the Eternal Buddha by calling the mandala *hoben*, an expediency or device that can be abandoned when it no longer serves its purpose.[26] *Hoben* frees Rissho Kosei-kai to shift in any direction that is felt to be best, therefore very extensive cooperation with other religions is perfectly fitting. It is equally fitting, however, for Soka Gakkai to appeal to this teaching to justify its mission methods, which are certainly *hoben* in the sense of being effective in bringing in new members. *Hoben* is significant for Rissho Kosei-kai in the sense that it is a teaching that makes change congruent with the *sutra*.

The other passage in the *Lotus Sutra* that is important in this connection is the Eternal Buddha theme in chapter 16. This passage is useful to support the notion of cooperation with other religions. Sakyamuni here discloses that he is not just a man but that he is the Eternal Buddha, who has always been. He is thus the ultimate Reality, not just one religious leader among others. One passage expresses this in the words of Buddha:

> If in other religions there are beings,
> Reverent and with faith aspiring,
> Again I am in their midst.[27]

This notion becomes the explicit basis for a cooperative attitude toward other religions, for it can be understood as a sort of universalism. Buddha is in all religions, no matter what name is given to him. He is the Reality behind the words and forms of all religions.

2. A second major element in the cooperative stance of Rissho Kosei-kai lies in factors in its history that have involved it with other religions. President Niwano himself, while a diligent student of the *Lotus Sutra*, has had little technical training in Buddhist doctrine. His background includes many influences from folk religion, such as divination, onomancy, and faith healing.[28] His motivation has not been to preserve any particular traditional doctrines, but to help people. He has tended, therefore, to draw on any practices that are helpful, regardless of whether they came from Buddhism or folk religions. In this sense, *hoben* freed President Niwano to use ideas from other

religions so long as they helped people. Myoko Sensei, the woman who was the other major personality in the founding of Rissho Kosei-kai, was a charismatic type of person with many shamanic characteristics.[29] This type of leadership is not customarily found in traditional Buddhism but derives from the folk-religion motifs. Even when one operates within a tradition such as Buddhism, a shaman is relatively free of the restrictions of the tradition, because a shaman receives guidance directly and immediately, rather than through institutional forms or traditions. Thus both of the founders of Rissho Kosei-kai can be seen as drawing from the folk-religion motifs. They felt value in them and thus tended to be more open toward them.

An additional historical factor is implicit in the above, namely, that Rissho Kosei-kai has not been institutionally related to any Buddhist priesthood. It is an independent Buddhist layman's movement. Priesthoods have generally tended to be more self-conscious about doctrinal distinctions and differences than have laymen. Where such awareness of differences exists, it is more difficult to cooperate with other religions as fully as might be done if there were less sensitivity to details, which is more typical of laymen. Soka Gakkai has a much different history from Rissho Kosei-kai in this regard. Connected with Nichiren Shoshu as the layman's movement of the sect, it has been associated with a most uncooperative form of Nichiren Buddhism.[30] Soka Gakkai tends to be less cooperative in part because of its close association with the relatively uncooperative Nichiren Shoshu. Rissho Kosei-kai has no such association to inhibit cooperation.

3. A third major element in the cooperative stance of Rissho Kosei-kai is the personality of President Niwano. He, with Myoko Sensei, was the founder of the sect in 1938, and he continues as the central figure of the movement. He seems to be a kind of father figure for the entire group and has a broad appeal. His approach to other religions has a spirit of openness and acceptance about it. Something of his personal attitude can be sensed from the following passage, written shortly after he had met the Pope.

> I firmly believe that religious cooperation among Buddhists will lead to cooperation with Christianity in Japan too. This should be natural in view of the fact that in Rome an agreement was made at the conference

> with the Japanese bishops, and it also corresponds with the idea of the Pope. The great ideal of "religious cooperation" for which I have spent twenty-seven years of activity centering around Kōsei-kai, my forty years of religious life and the sixty years of my life, is now steadily going to be established.[31]

It may be that the impact of President Niwano's personality on the movement is even greater since the passing of Myoko Sensei. In the years since her death President Niwano has held the central position alone. In some ways the movement has passed beyond Myoko Sensei, who, while still honored, is seen by some as *hoben*.

There is a circular character to all of this. President Niwano's openness to other religions has led to close relationships with leaders in other religions, and these relationships have, for the most part, been happy ones. The fact that the leaders of other religions are men whom Niwano looks upon as friends encourages him to cooperate still further.[32]

4. A fourth major element in the cooperative attitude of Rissho Kosei-kai is found in what may be called socio-psychological factors. Some of them are related to elements mentioned earlier, but they all are part of the social and psychological situation in which Rissho Kosei-kai has come to its present form. At least seven points can be noted in this connection: (a) As mentioned above, Rissho Kosei-kai, unlike Soka Gakkai, is not related to a regular Buddhist sect. It does not have a priesthood or tradition that might limit religious cooperation. (b) The early attempts at cooperation were happy and profitable. As Father Stepfer of the Oriens Institute in Tokyo expressed it, Rissho Kosei-kai "sees a future in cooperation" based on its past experiences.[33] (c) Group counseling, or *hoza*, which has been helpful in bringing members to Rissho Kosei-kai, is a practice possible in any religion. The result is that a number of scholars from the West have come to observe and study it to learn from it. This fact alone has brought about many contacts with other religions under the most favorable of conditions. (d) Becoming a member of Rissho Kosei-kai causes only a slight disruption of a new member's loyalties. It is not looked upon as a rejection of the religion of the family, and there is provision for ancestor veneration. Also, there is no rejection of Shinto practices relating to birth and marriage, so a member can keep the traditions

of the family and nation while still sharing in the new religion. A conciliatory attitude toward other groups is thus maintained. (e) Many of the new religions have felt a need for cooperation among themselves if they are to achieve a place of respect in Japan. These new organizations, by working together, have sought to gain the respect of the Japanese people. The pressing concern for peace has led to further cooperation between the new religions and Christianity.[34] It must be noted that Soka Gakkai has taken the opposite approach with amazing success. (f) The concern for a good public image has also fostered a cooperative attitude in Rissho Kosei-kai. It is generally easier for a movement to be accepted by the public if it stresses those concerns that it holds in common with other accepted groups. (g) In my judgment, there is a desire in Rissho Kosei-kai to dissociate itself from some of the activities and attitudes of Soka Gakkai.[35] There are two issues that make this clear: its explicit opposition to the formation of religiously based political parties and its fosterings of, rather than opposing, cooperation with other religious groups.

5. The fifth element that enters into the cooperative spirit of Rissho Kosei-kai is the very content of its doctrines. There has been little effort to develop new doctrines. Rather, the teachings tend to be general and to have a practical bent. "Fundamental Buddhism" is an effort to unite as much of Buddhism as possible into one system, thus making it possible to cooperate with other Buddhists. The notion of Sakyamuni as the manifestation of the Eternal Buddha[36] who is in all true religion is surely favorable to cooperation with other faiths. The Buddha Nature is already in every man regardless of his religion and needs only to be "polished." Perhaps the general statement that best captures the doctrinal concern of the movement is that Kosei-kai seeks to recover "humanity"[37] in a world that seems to be losing it. These doctrines tend to have a universalism about them that makes it easier for the sect to cooperate with other religions, because the doctrines themselves establish some common ground and concerns.

A further fact is that the practical aspect of religion is stressed rather than the doctrinal one. Members are encouraged to "read with your body,"[38] which is the appeal to *act* in accordance with the dharma. It has been easier for Rissho Kosei-kai to cooperate with other religions because its concerns are not strongly doctrinal but have been largely for the improvement of the quality and conditions of human life, concerns shared by other religions as well.

This paper has attempted to show that Rissho Kosei-kai tends to be cooperative in its relationships with other religions and to indicate some elements that may contribute to the cooperative spirit. There is a need for a much more extensive investigation of these elements. It has also been noted that Soka Gakkai—which, like Rissho Kosei-kai, uses the *Lotus Sutra* and is related to Nichiren—is a most obvious example of an uncooperative religious movement. Some effort has been made here to note differences between Soka Gakkai and Rissho Kosei-kai that may contribute to the differing postures that they take toward religious cooperation.

NOTES

1. H. N. McFarland, *The Rush Hour of the Gods* (New York, 1967), p. 177.
2. *Rissho Kosei-kai* (Tokyo, 1966), p. 157.
3. *Ibid.*, pp. 29–30.
4. *Ibid.*, pp. 31–32.
5. *Kosei Times*, Apr. 1969, p. 1. At this meeting there were representatives of Buddhism, Shintoism, Roman Catholicism, Protestantism, Eastern Orthodoxy, Hinduism, Islam, Sikhism, Zoroastrianism, Judaism, and Unitarian-Universalism.
6. *Ibid.*, May 1969, p. 1.
7. *Ibid.*, June 1969, p. 1.
8. *Ibid.*, July 1969, p. 1.
9. *Ibid.*, Aug. 1969, p. 1.
10. *Rissho Kosei-kai*, p. 112.
11. *Ibid.*
12. *Ibid.*, p. 141.
13. An American student mentioned to several Soka Gakkai youth that she was with a program sponsored by Florida *Presbyterian* (italics mine) College and was greeted with ridicule and a fervent invitation to chant the *sutra* and receive the benefits that the students felt they had gained (Aug. 1969).
14. *Rissho Kosei-kai*, p. 141. On the conversion of members to Rissho Kosei-kai, see also E. Watanabe, "Rissho Kosei-kai: A Sociological Observation of Its Members, Their Conversion and Their Activities," *Contemporary Religions in Japan*, Vol. IX, Nos. 1 and 2, Mar.–June 1968.
15. M. Anesaki, *Nichiren: The Buddhist Prophet* (Gloucester, Mass., 1966), pp. 8 ff.
16. *Nichiren Shoshu Sokagakkai* (Tokyo, 1966), pp. 142, 203.
17. Anesaki, *Nichiren*, chaps. 9 and 10 passim.
18. Interview, Nov. 27, 1967. A similar observation was made by Professor Kubota of Rissho University.

19. *Nichiren Shoshu Sokagakkai*, p. 188.

20. McFarland, *The Rush Hour of the Gods*, p. 184.

21. *Rissho Kosei-kai*, pp. 43–79.

22. *Ibid*., pp. 27, 79. President Niwano notes that while Nichiren opposes Zen and Amida Buddhism, the *Lotus Sutra* does not (*Travel to Infinity* [Tokyo, 1968], p. 131).

23. *Rissho Kosei-kai*, p. 91.

24. The parable of the burning house tells of a father's deceiving his sons in order to get them to act wisely.

25. Interview, Nov. 27, 1967.

26. *Ibid*. See also *Rissho Kosei-kai*, p. 16, for more on the use of *hoben*.

27. *Lotus Sutra*, chap. 16, quoted in *Rissho Kosei-kai*, p. 94.

28. McFarland, *The Rush Hour of the Gods*, pp. 185, 189 ff.

29. *Ibid*., p. 188. See also H. B. Earhart, *Japanese Religion: Unity and Diversity* (Belmont, Calif., 1969), pp. 87 ff.

30. *Nichiren Shoshu Sokagakkai*, preface; McFarland, *The Rush Hour of the Gods*, p. 201.

31. *Rissho Kosei-kai*, p. 32.

32. Interview with Shuten Oishi, Secretary General of the Japan Religions League, Nov. 8, 1967.

33. Interview, Nov. 14, 1969.

34. *Rissho Kosei-kai*, pp. 110–11.

35. *Ibid*., pp. 32–33.

36. *Ibid*., pp. 76–77.

37. *Ibid*., p. 108.

38. Niwano, *Travel to Infinity*, p. 136. The phrase was originally used by Nichiren.

The Interpretation of the "New Religions" of Japan As New Religious Movements

H. Byron Earhart

In this essay the new religions of Japan *(shinkō shūkyō)* are examined briefly in terms of origin and definition in order to focus on their comparative significance.[1] The Japanese new religions arose as the result of three interacting factors: (1) the fossilization of the earlier traditions, (2) severe socioeconomic hardship, and (3) the creative inspiration of a founder. The new religions may be defined *chronologically* as those movements appearing from the early 1800's to the present; *in origin*, as those forces that thrusted toward renewal or revitalization; *in formation*, as those movements that constituted significantly new religious reorganization.

Scholarly opinion is in agreement on the fact that new religious movements constitute a common body of data, but there is no consensus on the general meaning of the data. Social scientists have opened up important dimensions of new religions, but their focus on religion as a function of culture in a crisis-response relationship leaves unanswered the question of the religious significance of these movements. However, if new religions are a common body of religious data, then we should be able to identify, analyze, and interpret the common structure of such new religions. This kind of "phenomenological" approach to the new religions results in a different understanding of their significance.

Reflection on other comparative studies and my own work on the Japanese new religions leads to this tentative phenomenology of new religious movements:

1. New religious movements presuppose a prior (or established or classical) tradition.

2. They involve a radical break therefrom (and not just an inner critique or reform).

3. The thrust of this break is toward renewal or revitalization.

4. This results in a significantly new reorganization (or gestalt).

Introduction

One of the most conspicuous developments in recent Japanese religious history is the large number of so-called new religions, *shinkō shūkyō* or *shin shūkyō* in Japanese. Although these new religions have attracted considerable scholarly attention, a preliminary review of Western-language literature reveals little common agreement on the interpretation of the origin, definition, and comparative significance of these religious movements.[2] All three problems—origin, definition, and comparison—are closely related, but they cannot be treated in full here. The two problems of origin and definition will be sketched briefly in order to ask about the wider comparative significance of the Japanese new religions. My general thesis is that a phenomenology of new religious movements is crucial to all three problems, but especially to the third. The thrust of this paper is theoretical and does not attempt to tap the vast historical materials dealing with the new religious movements outside of Japan.[3] In the investigation of basic methodological problems, various theoretical formulations will be critically evaluated.

Japanese New Religions: Origin and Definition

The historical origin—or origins—of the new religions have most often been seen in terms of a socioeconomic "crisis," causing the appearance of new religions, which then resolve the crisis. This kind of interpretation seems to be faulty both in its estimation of the relationship between religious and nonreligious activities, and also in its analysis of the new religions. These recent Japanese religious movements, like all religious phenomena, are complex in their historical development and present nature. In the case of the Japanese new religions, it seems that three interrelated factors help us understand their appearance. First, the major "established" religions (Buddhism and Shinto) had become so formalized or fossilized that the time was ripe for some form of renewal outside of the existing organized religions.[4] This prior religious history provided a two-pronged enabling factor: while directing the appearance of new religions as innovations external to organized religion (rather than internal reforms), it also supplied the general religious content for them. Second, severe socioeconomic hardship helped provoke the social crisis that raised the question of where people placed their real trust. This social unrest contributed a precipitating factor, in the sense of directing the timing of the new religions and, to a certain extent, in the sense of channeling the shape of the new movements. Third, charismatic leaders or semidivine founders either rediscovered a vital religious element from the previous tradition or received what they felt to be a new revelation. These founders and leaders offered the inspiration that was the point of orientation for a new religious movement. These three factors—the enabling and the precipitating as well as the inspiration—interacted as a group to create a number of rather distinct new religions.[5]

In defining the new religions the two basic problems are dating the emergence of the new religions and recognizing the features that set these movements apart as a distinctive phenomenon within Japanese religious history. Some of the new religions arose as early as the beginning of the nineteenth century, while some have been founded since 1945, the most flourishing period for the new religions. Some scholars date the emergence of the new religions with the appearance of those pioneer groups of the early nineteenth century, while other scholars insist that new religions (or "modern religions") did not really emerge until just before or after World War II. Each of these periods exhibits peculiar features worthy of consideration, but the question of chronology cannot be solved apart from the nature and scope of the new religions. Any interpretation of the nature of the new religions must embrace the total time span during which the new religions have been active.

The nature of the new religions must be understood in terms of their historical origin and time span as seen in the structure of their makeup. In general, "there seem to be three major criteria for distinguishing new religious movements: (1) chronologically, those movements that appeared from late Tokugawa [about 1800] or early Meiji [about 1870] to the present; (2) in origin those movements that arose as renewal or 'revitalizing' forces; (3) in formation, those movements that led to permanent socio-religious organizations."[6] These three criteria, when seen as three interrelated aspects describing a total phenomenon, are able both to embrace the total time span of the new religions and to indicate the general nature of the new religions. This definition allows the inclusion of any movements from late Tokugawa times to the present that are revitalistic in character and have resulted in socioreligious organization. This definition also permits the exclusion of essentially schismatic groups that separated from Buddhism and Shinto without erecting a distinctively new religious ethos. By virtue of the same definition we can exclude from the category of new religions those ethical and cultic activities that have not resulted in new socioreligious organization.

The Problem of New Religions as New Religious Movements

Now that we have considered the origin and the definition of the new religions, we can focus more closely on the problem of their wider comparative significance. One reason scholars have found it difficult to make generalizations about the Japanese new religions is that, on a wider scale, they were unclear about the generic nature of these new religions. Consequently, neither the generalizations about the Japanese new religions nor the wider kinds of comparison have been particularly fruitful.[7] Of course, any set of human phenomena can be compared and contrasted in a great many ways. The new religions, too, are human phenomena that can be treated on various levels, such as psychological, sociological, political, or economic. In actuality, these levels can never be completely separated; but another kind of question is, "What constitutes the religious character of these movements? Is there something that distinguishes "new religions" from other kinds of religious organizations? If we agree that these new religions are phenomena that have some characteristics in common, then we must be able to analyze and interpret that set of characteristics. In both the humanities and the social sciences—in fact, in any discipline—one must always ask what can be compared and what cannot be compared; then, among the various possibilities for comparison, one must ask which kinds of comparison best elucidate the material at hand.

It is my contention that the Japanese new religions will make more sense as a whole, and their comparison with other groups will make better sense, when these groups are treated in terms of their basic character as new religious movements. In other words, I am proposing a phenomenology of new religious movements. This proposition presupposes the existence of a great number of such new religious movements, appearing at various times and places and possessing a rather common structure. To my knowledge, no satisfactory phenomenology of new religious movements is available, but on the basis of my preliminary research into the Japanese new religions, I would like to suggest their significance for such an undertaking. In fact, a number of scholars have been investigating the same general problem area, and it is worthwhile to measure the results of their comparative studies over against the case of the Japanese new religions.

The concept of new religions or new religious movements has existed for some time, but lack of clarity has prevented it from gaining currency. In modern times, as early as 1913 the notion of new religions formed the topic of an article by the anthropologist Alexander F. Chamberlain, who wrote:

> One of the most interesting topics in the history of human civilization is the question of "new religions," and closely related phenomena. By "new religions" is here meant such religious ideas and movements, propaganda, etc., as spring up among more or less primitive or uncivilized peoples, particularly after their contact with the so-called "higher" races. The "new religion" is often largely, and sometimes almost wholly, the result of the suggestions of the religious ideas introduced by missionaries and other representatives of the intrusive culture.[8]

Chamberlain noted the presence of this kind of religious movement throughout the world, drawing his materials from primitive peoples, especially American Indians. The three features of this definition are quite interesting, particularly when considered in the light of the Japanese new religions. According to Chamberlain, new religions appear (1) among primitives, (2) particularly after contact with higher races, and (3) largely as a result of the religion of the intrusive culture. The case of the Japanese new religions proves that none of these factors is essential: (1) The Japanese are not a primitive people; (2) contact with a "higher" or other culture was not a major factor in the appearance of the Japanese new religions; and (3) the Japanese new religions were not primarily the result of the religion of an intrusive culture.

Now, even if Chamberlain did not know about the Japanese new religious movements, the contemporary scholars who treat the Japanese materials and quote Chamberlain do not call his definition into question; they invoke his article merely as another example on the level of crisis-response and mass movements. Even the work of Lanternari is based on a similar notion of intrusive cultures producing a religious reaction, except that Lanternari specifies that the intrusive culture is the Western world, either in political or religious domination. While we sympathize with Lanternari's humanitarian critique of Western colonialism, this notion is not helpful for developing a comparative definition of new religions. Lanternari's treatment breaks down, in fact, when it encounters the Japanese new religions—until 1945 Japan knew no colonial period or military occupation. Lanternari must radically alter his theme that the new religions were caused by the crisis of Western influence to the notion that they were caused by the crisis within Japanese society: "Japan had been seeking liberation, not from foreign rule but from forces within its own society."[9]

It may be noted that Lanternari's work and some other comparative studies do not necessarily focus on a definition of new religious movements, but they have continued the earlier attempt to compare recently emerging religious groups, particularly along typological lines.[10] However, more pertinent to the definition of new religious movements are the studies that attempt to embrace all such "types" into a general theory.

Anthropological and Sociological Interpretations of New Religious Movements

Those scholars who have made the most important systematic studies of new religious movements are the anthropologists and sociologists who have encountered newly emerging religious groups in various historical periods and geographical areas. These studies have considerable value for our present task, particularly because of their comparative inquiry and systematic plan. These studies are more concerned with the mechanism or process by which the new religions appear, and not with their religious character; nevertheless we can learn a great deal from these studies. A valuable critical interaction can be gained by a juxtaposition of these theoretical formulations with the case of the Japanese new religions.

The more recent literature often takes as its point of departure Linton's suggestion of "nativistic movements," which he defined as "any conscious, organized attempt on the part of a society's members to revive or perpetuate selected aspects of its culture." Linton tried to broaden the scope of earlier study of religious groups and to refine the explanation of their dynamics, but he still holds to the notion that cultural contact and "a situation of inequality between the societies in contact" are major causal factors in the emergence of religious movements.[11] Other scholars have pursued comparative and systematic studies but have criticized several aspects of Linton's suggestion. For example, Lowie has pointed out—quite perceptively, I feel—that messianic and nativistic movements need not necessarily emerge from cultural clash, but that "messianism springs from internal causes."[12] Another kind of critique of Linton's theory has been made by Worsley, who thinks that Linton overemphasizes the regressive aspects of these movements.[13] Marian W. Smith, in reviewing some of the abundant literature on cult movements, makes the same kind of critique and proposes the more positive term "vitalistic" to distinguish organized attempts to incorporate elements from another culture rather than to exclude them.[14] These criticisms of Linton's theory reflect a common tendency to seek out a more inclusive and systematic concept of new religious movements. Both kinds of criticisms—insistence on recognition of internal as well as external causes, and the need for a more positive appreciation of the thrust of such movements—are reinforced by the phenomena of the Japanese new religions.

Revitalization Movements

Among the various attempts to build these insights into systematic theoretical statements, we may select the works of Wallace and Smelser, and their respective formulas of "revitalization movements" and "value-oriented movements." These theoretical statements are particularly significant for focusing on the positive thrust of these groups as renewal forces and for sharpening the criteria by which the form of such religious movements can be recognized. Wallace uses the term revitalization to include all innovations in cultural systems, such as nativistic movements, reform movements, cargo cults, and messianic movements. "A revitalization movement is defined as a deliberate, organized, conscious effort by members of a society to construct a more satisfying culture."[15] Wallace makes an important distinction between usual cultural change, when there is a "gradual chain-reaction effect," and revitalization movements, in which cultural elements "are shifted into a new *Gestalt* abruptly and simultaneously in intent." I think that Wallace's idea of a changing gestalt marks a significant advance beyond the narrower theories of nativism and vitalistic movements; what identifies the Japanese new religions, too, is a new socioreligious configuration.

Some other aspects of Wallace's theory are not supported by the material of the Japanese new religions and the idea of new religious movements. Wallace not only defines revitalistic movements as including all the specific varieties of new religious movements, but he also treats them as "recurrent features in human history," in which almost all men participate. According to Wallace, both Christianity and Mohammedanism, and possibly Buddhism as well, originated in revitalization movements. Even myths and dreams are seen as possibly originating from personal and social revitalization processes. In effect, Wallace stretches the theory of revitalization so much that it becomes a total explanation for religion—the origin of religion, the emergence of myths, the conversion experience, and also the radically changed gestalt of a new religious group. But if revitalization becomes a total theory of religion, then it loses its potential for defining new religious groups. What Wallace really seems to be saying is that revitalization is the major characteristic of religion in general, and not of new religious movements in particular. If Wallace's theory of revitalization is to apply to new religious movements (and if it is to be internally consistent), the revitalization motive must be directly linked to the result of a new gestalt.[16]

Wallace has also specified some of the basic presuppositions of his revitalization theory. "The term 'revitalization' implies an organismic analogy," which in turn utilizes the corollary of the principle of homeostasis—a society works to preserve its own integrity or "life-supporting matrix" and, under stress, will act "to preserve the constancy of the matrix." Stress is a threat to the society and to the person's mental image of society ("the mazeway"), which results in changing the total gestalt or mazeway. This theoretical framework raises specific problems for the idea of new religious movements, but since the same problems arise in the background of Smelser's theory, comments on it may be reserved until after we have sketched Smelser's contribution.

Value-oriented Movements

Whereas Wallace attempts to treat cultural innovation and the roots of all religion, Smelser is concerned with collective behavior in general, setting apart religious or "value-oriented behavior." But Smelser's work is similar to that of Wallace, because he attempts to include the whole range of new religious movements, presupposes the behavioral model of homeostasis, and utilizes a wide range of religious data to support his argument. According to Smelser, "a value-oriented belief envisions a modification of those conceptions concerning 'nature, man's place in it, man's relation to man, and the desirable and nondesirable as they may relate to man-environment and interhuman relations.'" In general, "this regeneration of values is the identifying characteristic of a value-oriented belief," and "a value-oriented movement is a collective attempt to restore, protect, modify, or create values in the name of a generalized belief."[17] Smelser uses the notion of a value-oriented movement to include all of the same phenomena to which Wallace refers, and the wide documentation places it in the same category as our use of new religious movements. It is apparent that Smelser is singling out a particular kind of religious movement, for he points out that "not all religious movements are value-oriented," illustrating this with the comment that "the mere diffusion of new rituals into a religion does not necessarily require a full-fledged value-oriented movement."[18] Although Smelser uses different language, he, like Wallace, is insisting that some religious movements are distinguished by their formation of a new gestalt (which he calls a "value-added process"). Both the material of the Japanese new religions and a general concept of new religious movements lend support to this formulation.

A more problematic aspect of the theories of Wallace and Smelser is their basic cultural model, which seems to overemphasize the factors of equilibrium and stress and to deemphasize the symbolic significance of religious phenomena. Smelser's theory is similar to that of Wallace not only in identifying the form of the new religious movement but also in locating the origin of these movements in some stress that upsets prior equilibrium. "Value-oriented beliefs . . . arise when alternative means for reconstituting the social situation are perceived as unavailable."[19] Smelser is careful to include all the factors in the production of a value-oriented movement, since "any correlation between any type of deprivation and any type of value-oriented movement, then, must be assessed as part of a *system* of operating variables."[20] But even if the various factors are accounted for, the question remains as to whether or not the crisis-response (or equilibrium–stress–new-equilibrium) theory is appropriate for interpreting new religious movements.

New Religious Movements: Social Crisis and Symbolic Renewal

In general, both Wallace and Smelser have greatly advanced the theoretical consideration of new religious movements in their recognition of both the positive thrust of these movements and the major new gestalt that they constitute. However, if their theories are to contribute to a concept of new religious movements, these theories must be modified in two respects: by placing the crisis-response aspect in proper perspective and by giving full recognition to the symbolic significance of these movements.

Special attention should be paid to the "crisis" theory of new religions, particularly since it has been adopted by some students of religion in their interpretation of these movements. This notion is founded in the analogy of homeostasis—an equilibrium interrupted by strain and then brought back to a new equilibrium by a new religious movement. But this analogy has been questioned implicitly by the work of some scholars, including the anthropologist Stanner. In his treatment of cargo cults, Stanner notes that these cults provoke their own crisis—the impending event awaited by the new cult.[21] In brief, the new religion itself can easily, and often does, provoke a new crisis. To take an extreme example, there are reports of converts to the Japanese movements of Sōka Gakkai who have smashed the family altar, destroyed the family solidarity, and upset business colleagues in the endeavor to convert them.[22] To be sure, from the viewpoint of these converts, they are trying to impose a new (the only and true) mazeway; but from the viewpoint of the family (and society?), these actions represent a critical threat. Herein is seen a question of the relative importance of equilibrium and revitalization, a question wider than any particular family.

It may be noted that every theory has its special strengths and weaknesses. The equilibrium–crisis–new-equilibrium theory is strong in accounting for cultural order and continuity, but weak in accounting for regeneration. Why should we view the cultural organism only as striving for equilibrium? Why should we not also view the cultural organism as striving for regeneration? Obviously these questions cannot be answered in an either-or fashion, but my own acquaintance with new religious movements leads me to conclude that their dynamic thrust toward regeneration or revitalization has been neglected at the expense of overemphasizing the factor of return to equilibrium. This overemphasis is seen in the fact that equilibrium is treated as a permanent, positive goal, whereas revitalization is treated as lacking direction or goal, being simply the inevitable response to a lack of order and equilibrium.[23]

A side issue in this discussion is the question of the nature of religion and the dimension of crisis in religiosity.[24] Although this large problem cannot be treated in full here, it is worth noting that, of course, all religion deals with a critical dimension of life. All religious activity—potentially or actually—involves the human crisis of basing one's life on what is sacred or ultimately real—what we may call generally an existential decision. And when there arises a crisis that cannot be met by the present religious tradition, this situation does define a critical juncture for the old tradition and the opportunity for a new tradition. So the concept of "crisis religions" is not without basis, but it does contain two liabilities. One liability is practically the same as that found in Wallace's elaboration of revitalization: If the factor of crisis is treated as the generic quality of all religious forms, then it loses its ability to locate new religious movements. The second liability (which seems to diminish the theories of Wallace and Smelser) is more serious: failure to recognize the crucial symbolic character of new religious movements.

Stanner helps us avoid the first pitfall by proposing "that

we are dealing with phenomena of crisis necessarily having a religious form."[25] This is quite significant, because he has effectively related the factor of crisis to the emergence of a new religious movement (cargo cults) and at the same time has recognized that the result has the nature of a religious form. Stanner provides the needed modification of Wallace's and Smelser's theories, because the interpretation of religious movements simply as the response to crisis does not recognize that the revitalization or new gestalt "necessarily has a religious form." In other words, their theories do not take into account the symbolic content of new religious movements. I say "symbolic," because what is at stake in the theories of revitalization and regeneration of values is a major transformation of symbolic systems. What is lacking here is sufficient recognition that man always defines himself symbolically; therefore a new symbolic system is not a substitute for another kind of cultural or social activity.[26] It would be more appropriate to say that the totality of man's culture is a complex symbolic structure, part of which is religious symbolism that should not be mistaken for merely social symbolism. By symbolism I mean those images by which man experiences the world and defines his life in the world. Man participates in a number of interrelated symbolic systems that, as a whole, define his world view. When interpreting either one internal symbolic system or the total world view, the respective symbolic unities must be honored. Geertz has effectively recognized the necessity of studying religious materials as symbolic systems, but no one has applied this insight to the study of new religious movements.[27] This insight must be verified in the analysis of actual religious movements, and in future research I hope to take up this task with Japanese new religions. But for the moment this insight can be stated theoretically by expanding Stanner's statement to read: "We are dealing with phenomena of crisis necessarily having a religious form of symbolic renewal." In other words, new religious movements initially emphasize renewal (rather than equilibrium), a renewal that searches for and makes claim to a new symbolic system that can resolve both the immediate crisis and also the critical or existential dimension of human life generally.

The Interpretation of New Religious Movements

Considerable attention has been paid to the crisis-response formula, because it has proven to be one of the major obstacles in the interpretation of the origin, history, and comparative significance of new religious movements. Now we must attempt a more constructive treatment of new religious movements, which takes into account their symbolic character. An adequate interpretation of new religious movements must be able to hold together in proper relationship (1) a definition of the nature of religion, (2) the location of the juncture of new religious movements, and (3) an explanation of the continuity of religious forms (and cultural forms).

Religion is that mode of life or symbolic activity by which man discovers, expresses, and celebrates what is ultimately meaningful to him. Religion is always directly related to every other aspect of life, but it focuses on what is ultimate, real, or sacred. The concrete forms of religious life vary according to their particular context—that is, they are relative to where they appear; and they maintain a modified continuity through time—that is, religious forms are handed down as traditions that are undergoing modification.

The element of renewal (or rebirth or regeneration) is found in all religious traditions, because in the celebration of the power of the sacred lies the possibility for transforming mere physical life into human and transhuman planes. One of the best examples of the theme of birth and rebirth is found in initiation rites, but it is a universal religious theme.[28] Religious traditions are handed down so long as they remain vital and continue to provide participants with a meaningful orientation in life. But the time comes in almost any tradition when the original inspiration fades and religious forms are practiced and transmitted without recreating the original inspiration. This state of affairs can be called formalism, stagnation, or fossilization. At these junctures the "time is ripe" for renewal, and new religious movements appear. Of course, the process of fossilization and renewal is going on in every tradition at every moment in the continuing modification that affects the way in which the tradition is handed down. However, at particular junctures the whole tradition is significantly reorganized into a new socioreligious organization (or new gestalt), which constitutes a new religious movement.

Every religious tradition represents a continuity in time, which is identifiable by virtue of the forms and goals that are crucial to it. This continuity can be traced by following the succession of a set of interrelated ritual, ecclesiastical, and soteriological forms. On the one hand, this continuity holds even in the face of the emergence of new religious movements. On the other hand, the emergence of new religions marks a significant break from the preceding orderly succession.[29] A new religious movement does not necessarily introduce new content, but it must constitute a significant reorganization. For example, Japanese religion manifests a continuity from ancient times to the present, in spite of the appearance of the new religions. The new religions incorporate some fairly novel elements, but on the whole they preserve the persistent themes within earlier Japanese religion.[30] What the Japanese new religions have accomplished is a significantly new kind of socioreligious organization in contrast to the former pattern of Shinto shrines and Buddhist temples. Therefore, there is no contradiction between the idea of "new" religious movements and insistence on the historical continuity of religious traditions.

A Tentative Phenomenology of New Religious Movements

Having reviewed some of the literature on new religious movements and the major problems of interpretation, I will now venture a tentative phenomenology of new religious movements, based particularly on my familiarity with the Japanese new religions. In the first place the very idea of a new religious movement presupposes an established tradition from which or in opposition to which the new group emerges. In Japan there is the specific term *kisei shūkyō* (established religion); but even in the case of new religions among American Indians we can see clearly the contrast between the "classical" tribal tradition and such renewal movements as the Ghost Dance Religion.

In the second place, a new religious movement constitutes a significant break from the prior, or established, tradition. A new religious movement is to be distinguished from internal reforms, whether they are revisions of liturgy or polity. For example, changes in Roman Catholicism such as the vernacular mass or even a married clergy do not necessarily constitute a new religious movement. Schisms, too, are of a different category, simply implying a new authority.

In the third place, the thrust of the break is toward renewal or revitalization. The implicit or explicit criticism of the old tradition is its inability to speak to present-day people. Whereas social scientists may emphasize the crucial importance of a crisis situation, such a crisis will not provoke a new religion unless the old tradition is incapable of handling it. (Sometimes crises—such as the martyrdom of early Christians or the World War II bombing of London—can strengthen faith.) Revitalization necessarily implies the decline of the prior tradition. Therefore, it seems to me that the concept of revitalization makes sense only in a pair of terms, such as stagnation and revitalization. A renewal or revitalization movement promises literally a new life, a new access to religious power.

In the fourth place, the thrust of renewal results in a new socioreligious organization. It is true, of course, as Wallace has pointed out, that revitalization is a recurrent feature of all religions. However, a revitalization movement is distinguished when renewal is incorporated in a significant reorganization (that is, in a new gestalt): a new configuration has appeared. There is no need to look for new religious content, because what is important is not the relative balance of old and "new" elements, but the resulting new socioreligious movement.

This phenomenology of new religious movements is still tentative, requiring further verification from Japanese and other examples.[31] Nevertheless, it is hoped that the elaboration of this phenomenology will help both to clarify the particular context of the Japanese new religions and to raise comparative questions. This kind of comparative study always involves scholarly cooperation, and it is hoped that others interested in the problem will contribute their own materials and theories toward a more inclusive interpretation of new religious movements. Of greatest significance is the fact that these movements are not merely responses to crisis or substitutes for other forms of action; they are attempts at religious renewal, through which the forms of religion again help people define their world and their careers therein.

Retrospect, 1973

This article was written in 1969 and retains essentially its original form, except for minor revision of footnotes. During the past few years a number of books and articles on the Japanese new religions have been published, but it would require another article to treat them thoroughly.[32] Suffice it to say at this point that the main thesis of the article is still relevant today. Although there is even more scholarly interest in the new religions, still no generally accepted interpretation has been reached. The most widely used theory for studying the new religions is some form of the crisis (or anomie) explanation. In my estimation this theory is not adequate for comprehending the basic problems of the origin, definition, and comparative significance of these new religious movements. My own phenomenological approach is an attempt to resolve these issues by balancing the various factors rather than using one factor as the major explanation. What is needed now is a demonstration of this theory through a comprehensive analysis of the new religions. Obviously this is a large task and can be completed only by the cooperation of a number of scholars who will have to further innovate if a generally accepted theory of new religious movements is to be achieved.

NOTES

1. This paper was read at the national meeting of the American Academy of Religion, Oct. 17, 1969, and was published in Japanese translation in *Nihon Bukkyo*. Research for this paper was supported by Western Michigan University through a Faculty Research Grant and by a Study and Travel Grant to Japan from the Institute of International and Area Studies; grateful acknowledgment is also made for a 1969 summer stipend from the National Endowment for the Humanities.

2. H. Byron Earhart, *The New Religions of Japan: A Bibliography of Western-Language Materials*, a Monumenta Nipponica Monograph (Tokyo, 1970). Hereafter this work is referred to as *New Religions Bibliography*.

3. See *New Religions Bibliography*, app. C, "Comparative Materials for the Study of New Religious Movements."

4. For a brief analysis of "fossilization and renewal" in recent Japanese religion, see H. Byron Earhart, *Japanese Religion: Unity and Diversity* (Belmont, Calif., 1969), esp. pp. 69–98. Some friendly critics have voiced objection to the term fossilization, because it seems to have a pejorative connotation. However, the term is intended to be not pejorative but descriptive, indicating a tradition whose forms are preserved and whose ceremonies are practiced, but whose vitality is waning or almost absent.

5. This problem is treated at greater length in H. Byron Earhart, "The Interpretation of the 'New Religions' of Japan as Historical Phenomena," *Journal of the American Academy of Religion*, 37.3; 237–48 (Sept. 1969).

6. See *New Religions Bibliography*, p. 6; see also items listed under "definition of new religions" in the topical index for other attempts to interpret the new religions.

7. The same problems of method and interpretation seem to trouble works on the Korean new religions, which quote the "crisis" theory that has been applied to the Japanese new religions. Spencer J. Palmer writes that in spite of the diversity of Korean new religions, "nevertheless, all of these New Religions have emerged from a common socio-ideological tradition, and they have been generated and shaped by the sudden impingement of the same kinds of outside forces" (Spencer J. Palmer, ed., *The New Religions of Korea,* Vol. XLIII of *Transactions of the Korea Branch, Royal Asiatic Society* [Seoul, 1967], p. 2). This so-called crisis theory needs to be reexamined both on the theoretical level and in its application to historical materials. The present article criticizes the crisis theory primarily in terms of its applicability to Japanese new religions, but it is both necessary and fruitful to consider its implications for comparative study.

8. Alexander F. Chamberlain, " 'New Religions' Among the North American Indians, Etc.," *Journal of Religious Psychology,* 6.1:1–49 (Jan. 1913).

9. Vittorio Lanternari, *The Religions of the Oppressed: A Study of Modern Messianic Cults,* trans. Lisa Sergio (New York, 1965), pp. 223–27. See also the reviews in *Current Anthropology,* 5.4:447–65 (Oct. 1965). Another modern scholar who tends to follow Chamberlain is H. Neill McFarland, *The Rush Hour of the Gods: A Study of New Religious Movements in Japan* (New York, 1967); see esp. pp. 14–15.

10. See, for example, Guglielmo Guariglia, "Prophetismus und Heilserwartungs-Bewegungen als völkerkundliches und religions-geschichtliches Problem," *Wiener Beiträge zur Kulturgeschichte und Linguistik,* 13:1–322 (1959).

11. Ralph Linton, "Nativistic Movements," *American Anthropologist,* 45: 230–40, esp. 230 (1943).

12. Robert Lowie, "Primitive Messianism and an Ethnological Problem," *Diogenes,* 19:62–72, esp. 65 (Fall 1957).

13. Peter Worsley, *The Trumpet Shall Sound: A Study of "Cargo" Cults in Melanesia* (2d, augmented ed.; New York, 1968), pp. 472–76.

14. Marian W. Smith, "Towards a Classification of Cult Movements," *Man,* Jan. 1959, pp. 8–12. Smith is already commenting on Wallace's notion of revitalization.

15. Anthony F. C. Wallace, "Revitalization Movements," *American Anthropologist,* 58:264–81, esp. 265 (1956). See also his reply to Smith, entitled "Towards a Classification of Cult Movements: Some Further Contributions," *Man,* Feb. 1959, pp. 25–26. In his *Culture and Personality* (New York, 1961), pp. 143–44, there is a slightly modified definition of revitalization: "deliberate, organized attempts by some members of a society to construct a more satisfying culture by rapid acceptance of a pattern of multiple innovations." Wallace has elaborated his position somewhat in *Religion: An Anthropological View* (New York, 1966), pp. 30–39, 157–66, 209–15. See also his pamphlet *Religious Revitalization: A Function of Religion in Human History and Evolution* (Boston, 1961).

16. Even in Japan we find the tendency to compare new religions to the early or the "new" stage of Buddhism and Christianity. It is obvious that a religious tradition varies considerably from its earlier to its later stages, but this does not necessarily constitute the earlier stage as a new religion. See Akio Saki, *Shinkō Shūkyō—Sore o Meguru Gendai no Jōken* (The new religions—the contemporary conditions surrounding them; Tokyo, 1960), pp. 52–53.

17. Neil J. Smelser, *Theory of Collective Behavior* (New York, 1962), pp. 120, 122, 313.

18. *Ibid.*, p. 318.

19. *Ibid.*, p. 325.

20. *Ibid.*, p. 347.

21. W. E. H. Stanner, "On the Interpretation of Cargo Cults," *Oceania*, 29:1–25 (1958). After this article was written, there came to my attention the recent work by Palle Christiansen, *The Melanesian Cargo Cult: Millenarianism As a Factor in Cultural Change*, trans. John R. B. Gosney (Copenhagen, 1969). Christiansen, too, in reviewing interpretations of cargo cults, calls into question both "Frustration and Stress Theories" and "The Deprivation Theory." At several major points my argument is in agreement with Christiansen (who criticizes overemphasis on factors external to the culture where such movements arise and who asks for more study of the factors inherent in the culture).

22. Anthony F. C. Wallace, *Religion: An Anthropological Review*, p. 30, states that "new religions, far from being conservative, are often radically destructive of existing institutions, aiming to resolve conflict not by manipulation of the self but by manipulation of the real world." In the first half of this statement Wallace recognizes the potentially disruptive aspect of new religions, but in the second half he attributes this potentiality to the shift from the personal to the "real world." In short, he does not seem to recognize the symbolic character of both the personal and "real" worlds, whether the attitude be conservative or otherwise.

23. Christiansen, *The Melanesian Cargo Cult*, p. 126, notes that "whether the individual author sees the cargo cult as a positive or a negative phenomenon depends, as stated previously, on whether he regards social and cultural change as a normal or abnormal process." Elisabeth Tooker has argued effectively against Wallace's theory that revitalization is due to disorganization. Analyzing Wallace's main example of the Handsome Lake religion, she concludes that "the explanation for the introduction of the New Religion of Handsome Lake is not to be found in the gross disorganization of Iroquois society at the time, but in the specific changes in the society, some of which have been interpreted as evidence of disorganization." See her "'On the New Religion of Handsome Lake," *Anthropological Quarterly*, 41.4:187–200, esp. 190 (Oct. 1968).

24. Christiansen, *The Melanesian Cargo Cult*, p. 125, in concluding his criticism of crisis theories, states that "all these points of view are the expression of functional explanations, the roots of which go back to Radcliffe-Brown, who regarded the new religions in the traditional societies in Africa and Oceania as an attempt to 'relieve a condition of social dysnomia.'" See A. R. Radcliffe-Brown, *Structure and Function in Primitive Society* (New York, 1965), pp. 183–84. See also Wallace's critical comments on functionalism in *Religion: An Anthropological View*, p. 38.

25. Stanner, "On the Interpretation of Cargo Cults," p. 21.

26. Smelser, *Theory of Collective Behavior*, p. 325, holds that "value-oriented beliefs . . . arise when alternative means for reconstituting the social situation are perceived as unavailable."

27. Clifford Geertz, "Religion As a Cultural System," in *Anthropological Approaches to the Study of Religion*, ed. Michael Banton (New York, 1966), pp. 1–46. Burridge argues Geertz's theoretical point in a concrete situation by insisting on the significance of symbolic representations in the cargo move-

ments. See Kenelm Burridge, *Mambu: A Study of Melanesian Cargo Movements and Their Social and Ideological Background* (New York, 1970), pp. 272–73. In reviewing some of the crisis and revitalization theories, I have been intrigued by the fact that they neglect the rich field of new aesthetic movements. I suspect that the same critique of the homeostasis theory could be made on the basis of a study of new art styles. See Meyer Schapiro, "Style," in *Anthropology Today: An Encyclopedic Inventory*, ed. A. L. Kroeber (Chicago, 1953), pp. 287–312, esp. p. 287: "Style is . . . a common ground against which innovations and the individuality of particular works may be measured," by study of which the art historian can "account for the changes of style."

28. See Mircea Eliade, *Rites and Symbols of Initiation: The Mysteries of Birth and Rebirth* (original title, *Birth and Rebirth*), trans. Willard R. Trask (New York, 1965).

29. In other words, cultural continuity and renewal movements are not mutually exclusive. I am emphasizing the thrust for renewal, or regeneration, because it is essential for new religious movements.

30. See Earhart, *Japanese Religion*, pp. 5–8, for a description of six persistent themes in Japanese religion. The same themes are found in the Japanese new religions, as demonstrated in my article "The Significance of the 'New Religions' for Understanding Japanese Religion," *KBS Bulletin on Japanese Culture*, No. 101, pp. 1–9 (Apr.–May 1970).

31. See the adaptation of the revitalization theory to Japanese Utopian movements by David W. Plath, "The Fate of Utopia: Adaptive Tactics in Four Japanese Groups," *American Anthropologist*, 68.5:1152–62 (1966). See also the article by Koepping, who follows Linton's theory of nativistic movements and its categories in his interpretation of a Japanese new religion: Klaus Peter Koepping, "Sekai Mahikari Bunmei Kyōdan: A Preliminary Discussion of a Recent Religious Movement in Japan," *Contemporary Religions in Japan*, 8.2:101–34, esp. 132–34 (June 1967). Brief mention of Wallace's theory of revitalization is made in Dator's functional interpretation of Sōka Gakkai: James Allen Dator, *Sōka Gakkai, Builders of the Third Civilization: American and Japanese Members* (Seattle & London, 1969), pp. 128–31. Harold W. Turner has proposed the study of new religious movements in the context of "the encounter of a primal society and its religion with one or more of the higher cultures and their major religions." See his "A New Field in the History of Religions?" *Journal of Religion and Religions*, Vol. I, No. 1.

32. Works by Noah S. Brannen, James Allen Dator, Kiyoaki Murata, and David W. Plath are discussed in my "Recent Publication on the Japanese New Religions," *History of Religions*, 10.4:375–85.

4

Epilogue

Epilogue

Robert J. Miller
University of Wisconsin

"A wise man may seek here, there, and everywhere
Whence it has come, and whither it has gone,
Through every region in all directions,
But he cannot find it in its essential nature. . . ."
—*Lalitavistara*[1]

This volume constitutes a search for the essential nature of religious ferment in Asia. It has been an attempt to describe and analyze specific cases that may lead to understanding the processes of readjustment, reassessment, and either renewal or reaffirmation characteristic of all major religions in the world today. If we are, in fact, dealing with a world-wide phenomenon, then perhaps *it* is too complex to understand as a whole. As noted in the Editor's Foreword, simplification may destroy the messiness, the complexity, of the system under analysis. Analysis without simplification often seems to add to the complexity. Thus, the concentration on religious ferment in Asia (or, rather, only in parts of that area!) paradoxically raises another question of ferment—the *intellectual ferment* in academic disciplines concerned with analyses of various aspects of human behavior. *Do* we all share the perspective of the "scientific tradition," a "secular" approach to our subject? Are we really able to comprehend social orders in which religion equates with day-to-day activity?

Byron Earhart's final essay in this volume proposes a phenomenology of new religious movements. Earhart argues that what we have discussed elsewhere as reappraisal, readjustment, renewal and/or reaffirmation has as its end product a restructured ideology-cum-organization. "There is no need to look for new religious content, because what is important is not the relative balance of old and 'new' elements, but the *resulting new socioreligious movement*" (my italics).

Let us underline the emphasis on restructuring ideas and the attempt to realize them through a socioreligious movement. Earhart's refusal to adopt a category which eliminates the messiness of hyphenation is significant. Analytically, for any real system it is only theoretically possible to separate religion from the social and political spheres. We seem to be returning to the concept that, in many societies, religion permeates *all* aspects of life—in fact, that *it* is the source of most of the world's "models" for living. It is this traditional totality—as a system of ideas-cum-action—that forces development of an organizational form through which to remodel the "world." Remodeling occurs either through reaffirming the traditional "verities" or through selectively receiving and incorporating the "new" and the "old." Those organizations stemming from the nonscientific traditions and proposing a model based outside existing society we term *religious*. Conversely, *movements* that stress a particular way of life, even though based in religious values and models of the ideal world, we tend to call nationalistic, or communalistic, or simply political.

Religious ferment may indeed reflect the perception of attacks on a total way of life. Such ferment leads the organization or movement to contend for power to direct the life of the whole society or at least the total life of the particular group adhering to the organization. In contemporary societies, such power most often has a political base. Religion, either as organization or as the source of values for a movement, enters into the generalized ferment of politics. It struggles for men's allegiance to specific ideas and for loyalty to the ideas' interpreters. It contends with the state for personnel, for funds, for media—for sources of power. It may become the mechanism through which a group can participate *in* a society but, ideologically, not acknowledge themselves as *part* of that society.[2]

For any modern society that takes as its ideal the harmonious and integrated state, such an attitude poses many problems. It complicates the assimilation and absorption of divergent "subcultures" into a greater whole, a goal to which many developing nations are committed. Modernizing states and modernized political elites, espousing a new, secular world model, attempt to relegate religion to a personal, socially insignificant sphere of activity. The State as the representative of Society—the secular all-inclusive whole—takes over channels through which religious ideas traditionally became part of the "way of life." Education, taxation, social services, arbitration of morals, control of offenders, sanctioning of marriage, legitimization of rights and duties —areas in which formerly the religious leaders held control—all have fallen to the State. Small wonder then that even "new" religions and "new" religious movements seek their continuity in past traditions, to give legitimacy and attraction to their claim for power. And small wonder, also, that even "secular" leaders attempt to justify their new model of the world in similar fashion, or to contend that "religion should stay out of politics"!

If we look back on our essays and remember Sam Jordan, we may ask, Is it ever possible to divorce religion from politics, from economics, from social life? Jordan was *acting* some portion of religion by advocating a new perspective on work and interpersonal relations. A community—such as the Lamaists of Darjeeling District—*act* their religion by maintaining the relationship between Sangha and layman, monastery and community. An organization—like the Jana Sangh—translates religion into action by pressing for a ban on cow-slaughter in India—a ban that would apply not only to its adherents, but to *all* Indians regardless of *their* religious affiliation.

In short, unless religion is relegated to the realm of purely personal *thought*, or unless a religion provides *no* imperatives to behavior, it must encroach on politics. It must contend with the state or with "secular" governing personnel for the right to define the bounds of proper social behavior. Though we are dealing here only with "major" religions, the statement is applicable to organized religions in general. To paraphrase Clausewitz's statement about war and diplomacy: Politics is Religion continued by other means.

Contemporary politics paradoxically continues religion by means of "secularization." It strips traditions of their "sacred" aspects and uses them to link innovations with past practices. Certainly in most "modernizing" and "underdeveloped" nations, contemporary politics overtly accepts the scientific view of rationalism, natural processes, and the human ability to control one's own destiny. Faith in some power outside of man—indeed, in many cases outside of the nation or state—is considered to be a deterrent to the growth of analytical capacity. Yet, in translating the new world view into action, contemporary politicians (often inadvertently) lay the basis for religious ferment.

The advocates of faith, of forces outside Man, of a different perspective on nature, are slowly excluded from power and fight back. In the process, they in turn must adapt to or present alternatives to the new view of the "real world."

In this volume we have presented many illustrations of the ways in which such adaptations occur. Our emphasis has been on those who fight back, on the guardians of tradition, rather than on the "secularizers." Yet, if traditional religious certainties are under attack, the process we have described here suggests that Kees Bolle is correct when he says: "Secularization is a necessary process that makes room for what is newly felt to be the real world. This simply means that a full-scale religious renewal is not possible except through secularization."[3]

NOTES

1. Quoted in Wm. Theodore De Bary, ed., *The Buddhist Tradition in India, China & Japan* (New York, 1969).
2. Robert J. Miller, "They Will Not Die Hindus," *Asian Survey*, 7.9:637–44 (Sept. 1967).
3. Kees W. Bolle, "Secularization As a Problem for the History of Religions," *Comparative Studies in Society and History*, 12.3:251 (July 1970).